live for the future now

a study of 1 and 2 thessalonians

by Michael Martin

Adult Winter Bible Study
LifeWay Press
Nashville, Tennessee

how to become a Christian

The future and worry seem to go together. Mention the future and people start talking about their worries. The Books of 1 and 2 Thessalonians have a great deal to say about the future. These books encourage us to live for the future now and trust God instead of worrying.

If you've never trusted your life to God, you can do that right now. First recognize that you are a sinner and need God's forgiveness. This involves repentance, which means to turn from or change your mind about something. In this case you turn from sin to God because you have changed your mind about how to live. Instead of letting sin control your life, you want God to control it so you can live for Him.

Next, believe in Jesus Christ and what He did on the cross to provide salvation for you. This is sometimes referred to as placing your faith in Jesus. It involves making a commitment to Jesus, trusting Him to forgive you, and promising to live for Him.

Finally, confess your sin to God and ask Him to forgive you through Jesus Christ. If you ask, God will forgive you and you will be His child forever.

After this experience, you will want to tell others about it and get involved in a church. A pastor or another Christian leader will be glad to assist you.

Printed in the United States of America
© Copyright 1999 LifeWay Press
All rights reserved.

No part of this work may be reproduced or transmitted in any form or by any means, electronic or mechanical, including photocopying and recording, or by any information storage or retrieval system, except as may be expressly permitted in writing by the publisher. Requests for permission should be addressed in writing to: LifeWay Press; 127 Ninth Avenue North; Nashville, TN 37234-0175.

This book is a resource for Developing Teaching Skills course (LS-0053) of the Leadership and Skill Development category. It is also the resource for CG-0490 in the subject area Bible Studies for the Christian Growth category in the Christian Growth Study Plan.

Subject Heading: Bible. N.T.
Thessalonians—Study and Teaching
Dewey Decimal Classification Number: 227.81

ISBN: 0-7673-9362-7

table of contents

We believe the Bible has God for its author, salvation for its end, and truth, without any mixture of error, for its matter. The 1998 statement of *The Baptist Faith and Message* is our doctrinal guideline.

Unless otherwise indicated, Scripture quotations are from the NEW AMERICAN STANDARD BIBLE © copyright The Lockman Foundation, 1960, 1962, 1963, 1968, 1971, 1972, 1973, 1975, 1977, 1995 Used by permission.

from the editor

Recently many people have shown a renewed interest in their calendars. The turn of a new century and in particular the beginning of a new millennium have created great interest, concern, and fear about the year 2000. Some are interested simply because this year's calendar has so many zeroes. Others have expressed concerns about Y2K and all the problems that could arise within and as a result of computers. Still others have been fearful because they have heard much about the return of Christ and much of what they have heard is conflicting.

The Books of 1 and 2 Thessalonians were addressed to people with interest in, concern over, and fear about Jesus' return. Written to people in the first century, the message of these books will help those in the 21st century. That message, how to live for the future now, will comfort and encourage us about our future.

This textbook for the 2000 Winter Bible Study has several important features.

- Comments on the Scripture are comprehensive without being extensive and they are written to appeal to today's adults.
- Charts of related topics or summaries of keys ideas appear in each chapter.
- Maps, photographs, and/or art illustrations are employed throughout the book.
- Each section of the textbook chapters contains a series of questions. Some questions relate to Bible content, answers to which can be found in the designated Scripture passage. Reflective questions are based on the Scripture passage and call for in-depth thought. Application questions focus on the passage's present-day meaning for readers. Each set of questions, identified by the title "For Your Consideration," has at least one of each of these three types of questions.

The questions can be used either in individual or group study. Individuals can read the Scripture passage and the related textbook paragraphs and then work through the questions. Leaders can use the questions (and the two learning activities in each chapter) to generate group discussion. Leaders will find further commentary in the *Expository Notes on Live for the Future Now: A Study of 1 and 2 Thessalonians* (ISBN: 0-7673-9590-5) and further teaching ideas and aids in the *Resource Kit on Live for the Future Now: A Study of 1 and 2 Thessalonians* (ISBN: 0-7673-9591-3).

Michael Martin, professor of New Testament and Greek at Golden Gate Baptist Theological Seminary, wrote the textbook. He also wrote the commentary on 1 and 2 Thessalonians in *The New American Commentary* (vol. 33).

Wayne Ozment

CHAPTER 1

recognize your progress

Scripture Verses	**•1 Thessalonians 1:1-10**

I don't know his name but he walked by my house every day for several months. He looked about 55 years of age and I think he had a stroke. At first a young woman and a small child (perhaps his daughter and granddaughter) accompanied him. They walked slowly. He used a cane and struggled to keep up.

Over the months he began to walk progressively faster. His balance clearly improved. His daughter no longer walked with him. Then gradually it appeared he carried the cane more from habit than from dependence on it for balance. I wonder if he realized how much he had improved or if frustration with his ongoing problems blinded him to what he had accomplished.

Sometimes we have a hard time appreciating our progress. Improvement can come in small, unnoticed steps and our desire to be more or better frustrates us. Paul began 1 Thessalonians by thanking God for these Christians and the spiritual progress they had made. He then cited evidence of growth and told them others also had noticed their progress. By affirming their past success, Paul encouraged continued effort.

We too need to take a kind and hopeful look at ourselves. We are not perfect but we can celebrate the spiritual growth that has occurred in our lives. At the same time we can anticipate continued growth in the Lord. We too can give thanks to God because the work He has begun in us gives us confidence He will continue to work with and through us.

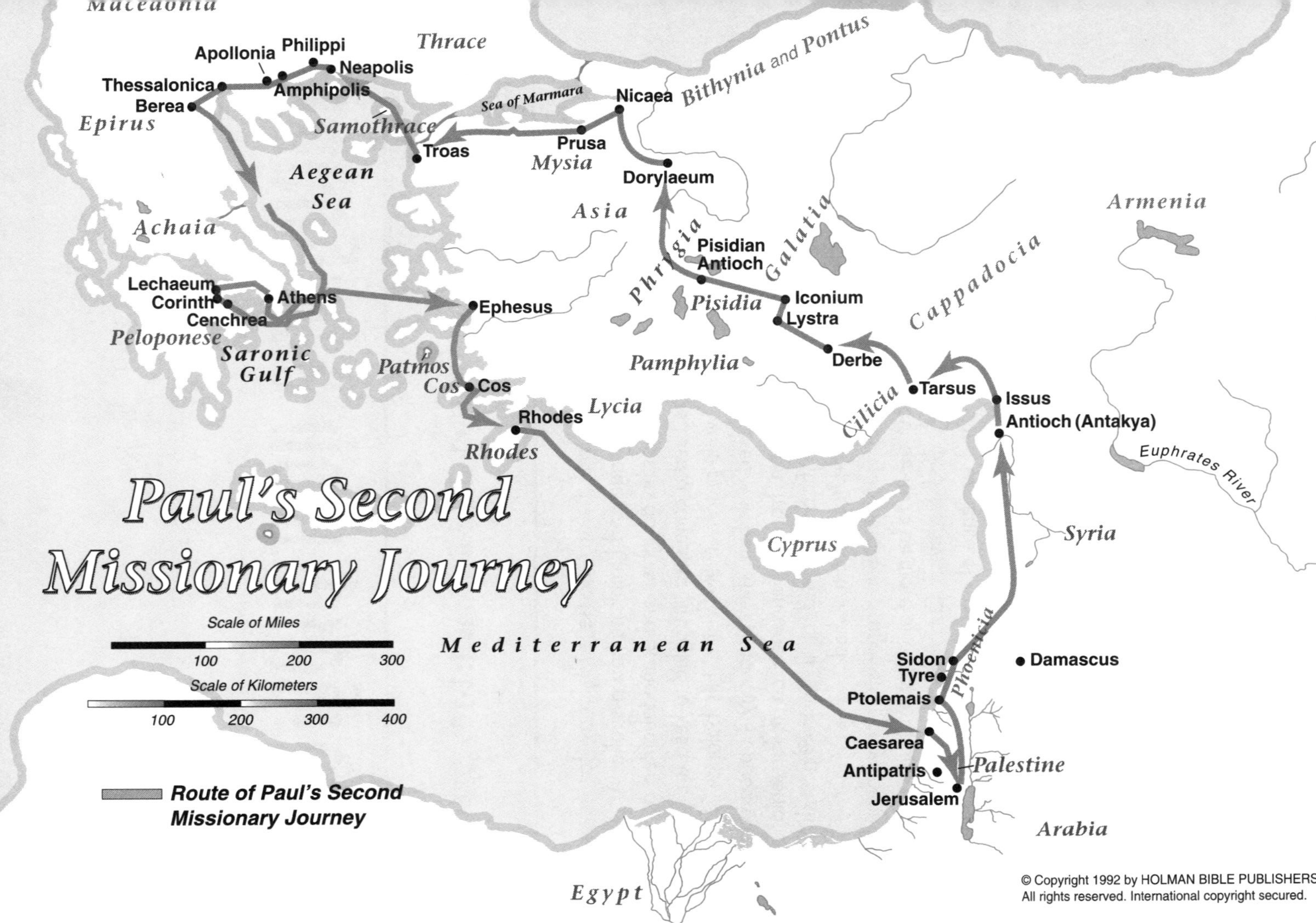

© Copyright 1992 by HOLMAN BIBLE PUBLISHERS
All rights reserved. International copyright secured.

Your Notes

(1 Thess. 1:1)

Greetings (v. 1)

Jesus changed the way Paul did the everyday business of life. Paul's Christian commitment affected even something so trivial as the way he addressed a letter. A personal letter in Paul's day normally began by naming the sender and recipients and by stating a brief greeting. Paul followed the conventional form but filled that form with distinctly Christian content.

"Paul and Silvanus [the longer form of the name *Silas*] and Timothy" established the church at Thessalonica (Acts 17:1-9). The Greek word for "church" means "assembly" and could be used of many types of assemblies. What distinguished this assembly from all others in Thessalonica? That which is true of any church! A church's distinctive is the members' shared commitment to the Father and the Son. Without this, the "assembly" is not Christian. In this commitment the members find unity and purpose and power.

For Your Consideration (1:1)

1. How does Paul's greeting in 1 Thessalonians 1:1 compare with his greetings in Romans 1:1,7; 1 Corinthians 1:1-3; and Galatians 1:1-3? SILAS + Timothy were included in I thess. Just Paul in the others

2. Why did Paul include Silvanus and Timothy as cosenders of the letter, and how do you imagine they shared this ministry?
They helped START This Church

3. How does your Christian commitment affect the way you conduct the simple everyday business of life, like greetings or letter writing?
I TRY TO Live my Life everyday with this committment A FACT.

Where a secular letter writer sent greetings, Paul extended "grace . . . and peace." Both are God's gift to His children. Through grace some benefit (in this case, forgiveness) is given to someone who does not deserve it. Peace translates the common Jewish greeting *shalom.* It implies an abiding sense of well-being, not just the absence of conflict.

A Good Beginning (vv. 2-5)

Charles was walking! His balance was erratic as he weaved his way across the room. But everyone was delighted. My eleven-month-old cousin had taken his first steps. He clearly loved being the center of attention. We praised his accomplishments. But even more, we celebrated the first steps of what we hoped would be a wonderful journey. Young believers deserve the same encouragement. Rather than focus on failings, we can celebrate attainment and encourage continued growth.

Paul assured the young church at Thessalonica he prayed for them regularly, thanking God for them. He then listed several reasons for his thanksgiving. First Paul expressed thanks for the "faith, love," and "hope" in this church.

Paul saw evidence of these three virtues in the lives of these believers. Their faith affected the way they lived. Their love compelled them to act in loving ways. Their hope enabled them to persevere through hard times. Their actions proved the reality of their commitment to Christ. When we see such proof in the lives of others, we too should give thanks to God and encouragement to others.

In the church's deeds Paul also saw evidence of God's movement. That God chooses His children displays His love for them. Paul was thankful for the mystery of God's love for sinners and His choice to make them His children.

The love of God gave birth to the gospel of Jesus Christ. Some respond to the gospel by rejecting it. For those who accept it, the gospel is the wisdom and the power of God (1 Cor. 1:18-24).

For Your Consideration (1:2-5)

1. For what did Paul express thanks in the Thessalonian church?

2. How did Paul describe the coming of the gospel to Thessalonica and what convinced Paul they were chosen children of God?

(1 Thess. 1:2-5)

3. When might acts of "love" be a "labor"? Why do you think Paul chose to link those two words?

4. Why do you think Paul complimented the Thessalonians so lavishly?

5. What in your life reveals your faith, your hope, and your love in a way that others can see?

6. Do you think all believers should mature to become witnesses and examples to others? Why?

Paul saw evidence of God's power in these believers in the presence of the Holy Spirit and in their "full conviction" about the gospel. The Thessalonian church, however, still had flaws (2 Thess. 3:6-15) and still faced struggles (1:6). But neither flaws nor struggles could obscure the wonderful fact of God's love, power, and presence in the church.

These truths were worth celebrating then as they still are today. Is there evidence of faith in Christ in your church? Can you detect God's presence? Are there signs of steadfast service? If so, you have a cause for thanksgiving and a basis for hope. Your church need not be perfect for you to celebrate the steps of faith you and others are taking. Learn to celebrate a good beginning even as you strive toward continued growth.

Amazing Growth (vv. 6-10)

How do you recognize spiritual growth? Acts of love and faith are signs. Steadfastness in the faith is another. The Thessalonians also revealed a growing maturity through their eagerness to follow Jesus' teachings. We can judge the level of Christian maturity in our lives by the same standards. The mature Christian is the one who lives out Christlike love, Christlike actions, and Christlike values.

Learning Activity 1

GRACE AND PEACE

1. What is grace?

unmerrited FAVOR

2. What is peace? CALM despite IN STORMS OF LIFE

3. How has God shown grace to you?

SAVed me

4. How has God shown peace to you?

gAVe it TO me

The new believers in Thessalonica became "imitators" of the apostles and of the Lord. An imitation sounds shallow to us. But for Paul the idea was a positive one. "Imitation" described disciples following the teachings and example of their master. It implied genuine devotion by true followers. The willingness of the Thessalonians to suffer "tribulation" for Jesus also proved their sincerity.

Paul, Silas, and Timothy served as living examples of what it meant to follow Jesus. Likewise, the Thessalonians' joyful dedication to Jesus made them examples of Christian commitment to their neighbors in Macedonia. News of their devotion to Jesus even traveled to the nearby province of Achaia.

Do you notice a pattern? As disciples mature, they become witnesses in word and deed. They model the meaning of Christianity and so reveal their own maturity as they demonstrate the meaning of discipleship for others.

A friend of mine was having trouble with his teenage son. As he searched for solutions, he discovered he himself was part of the problem. His son was not doing what he was told; he was imitating the behavior he saw. The father first needed to correct his own behavior. Are you a mature Christian? Can others learn Christlike living by seeing your life? Do they hear it in your conversation?

Paul's initial ministry in Thessalonica had been productive but difficult. (See Acts 17:1-14 for a description.) No wonder Paul praised the young believers' faithfulness in the face of tribulation (1 Thess. 1:6) and their perseverance despite all the "persecutions and afflictions" (2 Thess. 1:4) they had endured. No wonder believers far and wide told and retold the impressive story of the commitment and faithfulness of their brothers and sisters in Thessalonica. What an encouragement they must have been for others. And what encouragement they must have received by hearing Paul's words of recognition and praise.

Are you ever influenced by the opinions of others? Most of us are. Honest affirmation encourages the faithful. We too need to learn the value of honest praise. Paul shared words of encouraging praise. When was the last time you did the same?

For Your Consideration (1:6-10)

1. What signs of a vibrant, growing faith did Paul and others see in the Thessalonian church?

2. Why do you think the Thessalonians were able to endure the persecutions they suffered?

3. Which of the signs that the Thessalonians were growing in the Lord exist in your life?

4. What pressures are there in your community to serve other "gods" or live a non-Christian lifestyle? How do you deal with them?

Paul summarized the reports that circulated among other churches about the Thessalonians. First, he cited the nature of the "reception" the missionaries had in Thessalonica. Their visit was filled with turmoil, political threats, and real danger. Acts 17:9 indicates Jason even had to post a "pledge," probably something like a

Learning Activity 2

SAY A GOOD WORD

A young pastor invited an evangelist friend to preach a series of revival meetings at his church. When the meetings were over, the pastor took the evangelist to the airport. As the evangelist began to board the plane, he called back to the young pastor. His words—"Say a good word for the church!"

Three months later the young pastor received word that the evangelist had died. He thought of those last words he had heard from his friend. The young pastor committed his life to following the advice of the evangelist and spent the rest of his life "saying a good word for the church."

1. What good words do you want spoken about your church?

2. How well are you doing in speaking a good word for your church? (check one)

____ not very well ____ OK
____ good ____ very well

3. Are you satisfied with your response to the previous question? If not, what can you do to improve your attitude and/or actions?

peace bond that was guaranteed by the forfeit of money or property. For these believers, following Jesus required risking their reputations, their properties, and their relationships in the community. Yet many there believed, braved the opposition, and remained loyal to Paul and the gospel of Jesus Christ.

Even we who know so few details of the persecution in Thessalonica should be impressed. Would you alienate your friends and risk your possessions for the sake of the gospel? Would you alienate the government and risk legal prosecution by defending a missionary or your pastor? A faith that matures (sometimes quickly) to this level of commitment inspires us all.

Why did the Thessalonian believers risk all? These Thessalonians had given themselves over to serve the "living and true God." They served Him—not idols, not themselves, not others, not even Paul. Rejecting idols was not easy. Idols were an ingrained part of Greek life. Yet these new believers publicly stood against things their society mistakenly called normal and right.

Accepting the gospel also means believing the resurrection and looking forward to one's own. The gospel also anticipates the ultimate judgment of God on the error pagans call truth and the evil they call normal. Telling a world its ways are evil is never easy—even if the warning of judgment is balanced by the offer of salvation.

The gospel put the Thessalonians at odds with their past, their society, and their city's political and religious leaders. Yet opposition and persecution only served to highlight their commitment to the Lord. Their enduring commitment became a testimony and an inspiration to others.

Christians with a healthy and maturing faith live their testimony and inspire others to do the same. The report circulated in Paul's churches revealed an inspiring faith in Thessalonica. What kind of reports are circulated about you and your church?

CHAPTER 2

follow worthy examples

Scripture Verses	•1 Thessalonians 2:1-20

Christianity is caught not taught. Have you found this bit of popular wisdom to be true? Often we do learn by example. I still carry the impressions left on my life by a third-grade Sunday School teacher (Mr. Gurley), a pastor (Bro. Nardin), and a professor (Dr. MacGorman). Each in his own way lived the Christian life for me to see. I *caught* the faith from them (and others).

Yet these same men *taught* me the faith too. They took time to talk to me about their love for Jesus and the way it shaped them and their ministries. Their words revealed to me truths larger than any single act of faith could convey. For me, the faith has been both *caught* and *taught.*

Has God used both wise teachings and good examples to grow you in the faith? He did for the Thessalonians. Paul taught them about the faith. But he also lived a Christlike life among them. In his letter he encouraged them to imitate the Christian deeds and words they saw and heard from others.

Paul faced two difficult tasks.[1] First, he wanted to nurture the young believers in Thessalonica. By reminding the church of his behavior when he was among them (1 Thess. 2), Paul challenged the church to live for Christ as he had.

Secondly, Paul wanted to defend himself but only for the sake of the gospel. By slandering the apostle, opponents hoped to make the gospel appear false. Paul answered their charges with two ideas. (1) He lived so slander couldn't stick because it bounced off the evidence of his life. (2) He lived as an example of sincere faithfulness to Christ. What a great testimony! What a challenging goal!

Your Notes

(1 Thess. 2:1-6)

Be Bold and Genuine (vv. 1-6)

Paul was counting on these Christians' remembering what had happened when he and his coworkers came to Thessalonica. He could count on this because the time he spent there was not unproductive. Many had believed because of the missionaries' boldness and genuine faith. But these believers needed to do more than affirm the missionaries' testimonies. They also needed to live the same bold and genuine faith they had seen in Paul and his companions.

For Your Consideration (2:1-6)

1. Assuming Paul's denials reflect accusations his opponents had made against him, what were their charges?

2. How do you think Paul retained his confidence in God even after being jailed or run out of town by city officials?

3. In what situations have you ever lacked boldness as a believer? Why? What makes a person hesitant to witness?

4. If opponents tried to discredit your church's witness, what charges might they make?

Nobody wants to repeat a bad experience. During one of my first attempts at witnessing, an angry person gave two friends and me a tongue-lashing and virtually threw us out of her house. I did not enjoy the abuse. Had I been alone, I'm not sure I would have been bold enough to knock on the door of the next person on our list.

Paul had faced much harsher abuse in Philippi. Manhandled, publicly accused, beaten, and jailed, he finally was asked to leave town (Acts 16:16-40). Paul probably feared similar treatment in Thessalonica. But any natural fears he had did not stop him from sharing the gospel. Paul possessed boldness—not arrogance or blind self-confidence but a willingness to speak openly despite opposition. Paul's boldness began in his faith—he trusted God both with himself and with the consequences of his speaking the truth. Also Paul was bold because he knew he spoke the truth of God, not speculation.

TONY STONE

How can we become bold witnesses? Through the same divine source. Natural ability is good. Training is important. Experience makes witnessing easier. But true boldness grows only out of a close, trusting relationship with the Father.

Do you believe every salesperson who talks to you? If not, then which do you believe and why? If you are like me, you trust those who have proven their honesty. I check references. I ask friends if a certain business has treated them fairly. I look for a history that proves honesty.

Even bold witnesses fail to convince hearers if they are not believable. Paul knew this and reminded the church he had proved his genuine commitment to Jesus and his genuine love for them. Both Paul's words (preaching) and his behavior assured the church he had no dark ulterior motives. Paul was neither power-hungry nor greedy. Although he had authority as an apostle, he had not asserted his rights. For example Paul had the right but apparently refused to take financial support from the Thessalonians while evangelizing their city.

(1 THESS. 2:1-6)

Paul's actions proved his genuine commitment to the gospel. His deeds proved his genuine concern for the Thessalonians. Opponents could point to no evidence of greed or deceit in his dealings in their city. Can your church's neighbors say the same? Is the genuineness of your faith evident in your actions?

Be Caring and Encouraging (vv. 7-12)

I appreciate bold and genuine people. But I am especially drawn to those who are caring and encouraging at the same time. Boldness is a virtue but can be exercised in an uncaring way. Genuineness implies honesty; and speaking the truth is good, but honesty can be used as a club to embarrass or injure. A bold and genuine witness is most effective when given with a caring and encouraging spirit.

Paul's opponents may have argued that he did not really care about his converts and that in return they should no longer care about him or his message. Paul countered by reciting his actions among the Thessalonians. He tenderly cared for them as a

Learning Activity 1

WORTHY EXAMPLES

1. List individuals who have been worthy examples to you in your Christian faith.

2. How have these individuals helped you in your spiritual development?

3. How are you a better Christian because of their examples?

mother cares for her children. He was willing to pour out his life for them. He suffered hardship for them. He strove to live an example before them. He loved them like a father. Paul's example reminds us that caring Christians are gentle with other believers.

The tender love of parents for their child.

Paul's goal in working so hard was not personal advantage or praise. His goal was not financial gain. He labored so the Thessalonians might live in ways that please God. In other words, Paul's motives were selfless and holy. He worked for their benefit, not his own.

For Your Consideration (2:7-12)

1. How did Paul give evidence of his love for other Christians?

2. Why do you think Paul refused to burden the church, and do you think they appreciated his sacrifice?

(1 THESS. 2:7-12)

3. What evidence exists that you and your church love the new converts who are added to your fellowship?

Occasionally I serve as interim pastor for a church in the midst of conflict. I can help some of them specifically because I am an outsider. They know I am not a part of either side. Before I can make much of an impact, however, I have to prove that I care for them. Once they know I want only the best for them and their church, they usually are willing to listen—even to constructive criticisms.

Learning Activity 2

MINISTERIAL SUPPORT

Read Galatians 6:6 and 1 Timothy 5:17-18.

1. How do these passages support meeting the financial needs of missionaries and ministers?

2. Why did Paul not receive any funds from the Thessalonians?

3. How does your church assure its minister(s) that their financial needs will be met?

Be Faithful Witnesses (vv. 13-16)

Paul had suffered for the gospel, yet continued to stand as a witness. So had the church in Judea. They too were persecuted but continued in the faith. Likewise the church in Thessalonica had faithfully endured sufferings.

FOR YOUR CONSIDERATION (2:13-16)

1. What evidence did Paul have that his ministry in Thessalonica was not in vain?

2.. What had the opponents of the gospel done that would bring God's wrath on them?

3. What effects do you think persecution might have on your church?

4. What does the gospel's being the "word of God" mean to you?

Why did all these endure suffering? Why did they remain faithful to Jesus Christ? For one reason, they received the gospel as the "word of God." They recognized it was not human speculation, not just the teachings of the man Paul. The good news came from the one true God. Persecution could not change that truth.

Suffering for the truth is easier when you are not alone. The young believers had Paul's example to follow. They also knew of the faithfulness of the Judean churches and imitated them. They found strength and encouragement in the family of God and for this reason they too remained faithful.

Perhaps the Thessalonians also remained faithful because they knew the end of those who rejected and opposed Christ. Such people do not please God. They are "hostile to all men" since they hold needy humanity back from God who could meet their need. Ultimately these opponents of the gospel will face the wrath of God. Rejecting the path that leads to wrath requires remaining faithful to the truth that saves.

YOUR NOTES

(1 THESS. 2:13-20)

In Depth

As 1 Thessalonians 2 shows, genuine faith helps us overcome

a. fear of opposition (vv. 1-2)
b. slander by opponents (vv. 3-6)
c. human persecution (vv. 14-16)
d. satanic hindrances (vv. 17-20)

Believers today endure for the same reasons. Just as the Thessalonians needed the reminder and the example Paul provided, so those around you can benefit from your faithfulness. Resolve to stand as a faithful witness. Others will stand with you. And through us all the "word of God" will continue to work in power and love.

Persist Despite Problems (vv. 17-20)

Life is full of speed bumps, potholes, and unexpected detours. Smart travelers stay alert and flexible while moving toward their destination. Not even the apostle Paul was exempt from life's unexpected complications. Several times he had wanted to visit the Thessalonian church but each time Satan had hindered him.

FOR YOUR CONSIDERATION (2:17-20)

1. What did the Thessalonians, the Judeans, and Paul have to overcome in order to persevere in the gospel?

2. Why do you think believers should strive to maintain a nurturing relationship with young converts?

3. How might Satan hinder a ministry today?

We do not know what circumstance or person(s) Satan used to frustrate Paul's plans. But Paul assured the church his absence did not mean he did not care. Though Satan prevented Paul's physical presence, Paul found ways to persist in ministry to the church. His prayers, his letters, and the messengers he sent expressed his concern and continued his ministry.

Your ministry and mine do not always go as planned either. We cannot always meet the expectations of others. We sometimes find our best efforts frustrated. But Paul's example reminds us that all we can ever do is give our best effort to the Lord, persist despite problems, and depend on His power and wisdom for the results. Our persistence (not just our successes) provides a testimony and an example God can use to bless and challenge others to a life of faithfulness as well.

---

[1] I. H. Marshall, *1 and 2 Thessalonians* in *The New Century Bible Commentary* (Grand Rapids: Eerdmans, 1983), 60-61. Marshall debates the two possible contexts for chapter 2—but the two are not necessarily mutually exclusive.

keep on growing

Scripture Verses	•1 Thessalonians 3:1-13

I grew up in the home of a handyman. Dad fixed everything himself. Partly his pride and partly our budget prevented him from hiring professional help. Whatever the work—plumbing, electrical, carpentry, or auto repair—he did it.

Over the years I learned a lot by helping him. I learned not to be surprised when things break, wear out, or go wrong—that's the way life is for everyone; and I shouldn't expect my life to be an exception. I learned the value of well-informed friends who can provide just the right mix of advice and assistance. I found that accurate information, the right tools, and patient persistence can fix many things. I learned to avoid frustration by expecting complications.

Many of these lessons also apply to our spiritual lives. Accidents happen, plans break down, opponents interfere, relationships need mending, unexpected complications crop up—such things are a natural, unavoidable part of life. Learning to accept them and deal with them in a Christlike and constructive way is an essential part of maturing in the Lord. When we do this, hard times become the dark background against which the glow of our faith shines even brighter.

Expect Affliction (vv. 1-4)

Paul already had assured the Thessalonians that he cared for them. He wanted to see them again but had not been able to return to Thessalonica. Yet he knew the opposition the church faced, so he decided to send Timothy to their aid. Timothy had stayed in Berea (near Thessalonica) when Jewish opposition forced Paul to leave, but Paul had told Timothy to join him as soon as possible (Acts 17:13-15). Timothy rejoined Paul in Athens.

JERRY GAZA

While in Thessalonica Paul had warned the church that—like other believers—they would face affliction. Was Paul saying affliction is an inevitable result of becoming a follower of Jesus? Do all Christians suffer for their faith? If so, why and how often does it happen?

For Your Consideration (3:1-4)

1. Where did the Thessalonian church's afflictions and temptations come from?

2. What did Paul do to help the Thessalonians deal with affliction?

3. Does affliction discourage spiritual growth or encourage it? How?

YOUR NOTES

(1 THESS. 3:1-4)

4. How can you prepare to survive afflictions and temptations that believers experience?

5. What could you do to help others who face some hardship?

Paul assumed believers everywhere would suffer affliction because the gospel has opponents everywhere. He once had helped persecute believers and he too had suffered after he became a believer. Paul also knew from experience that the church in Thessalonica had opponents.

The place and opponents, the method and severity vary; but witnesses in a fallen world frequently face affliction. Paul knew this truth, and thus he warned the Thessalonian believers. He wanted them to grow to the point they could survive the difficulties. We can heed the warning as well. If we cannot avoid affliction, we can learn to understand and overcome it.

Progress requires overcoming obstacles.

LIFEWAY

Paul indicated he already had taught the Thessalonians about Christian suffering. He probably told them many of the same truths found in 1 Peter 1:6-9 and 4:12-19 and given in the chart "Principles to Remember When We Suffer as Christians" below on this page.

In Depth

Principles to Remember When We Suffer as Christians

1. We who share Christ's life also share His suffering.
2. Suffering as a Christian confirms that the world sees our Christian testimony.
3. Judgment is certain on those who persecute the faithful.
4. Persecution can test, confirm, and refine our faith.
5. The ultimate outcome of faith is an eternity sharing the joy and glory of the Lord's presence.

Timothy probably repeated Paul's teachings when he sought to "strengthen and encourage" the church (1 Thess. 3:2). Timothy's presence also helped this church. Suffering (even for a good cause) is painful; suffering alone is worse. Paul sent Timothy to stand with the church, not just talk at them. Which would you rather have in hard times—a wise word, a sympathetic presence, a helping hand—or a friend who could provide all of these? What do you offer people in pain?

As believers who live in a fallen world, we too will face difficulty. As we do so, some basic truths will help us. First, living for Christ does not make us immune to the evil that inhabits a fallen world. So we shouldn't be surprised when we suffer. In fact, some suffering comes as a direct result of living as a Christian. Following Christ can make us targets for those who oppose the gospel.

Second, we can find comfort and strength from knowing we do not suffer difficulty alone. The Lord is with us. Others can pray for us. Christian friends can stand with us. This truth also reminds us to minister to fellow Christians experiencing hardship. Are we willing to sacrifice the time and effort to comfort them? Can they count on our support and find hope in our encouraging presence?

Third, we can find hope in the future. Suffering affliction in this life is certain. But God's judgment on evil is just as certain. Certain also is the ultimate victory of the people of God. Paul didn't say "Pain is short, and joy is eternal"[1] but he could have. When we look at present difficulty in the light of future success, we discover a hope that gives strength and comfort. By growing in understanding, in our ability to minister to one another, and in our anticipation of God's future victory, we acquire the strength to deal with the difficulties that afflict us all.

(1 THESS. 3:1-4)

Learning Activity 1

Spiritual Exercises

Locate the eight spiritual exercises hidden in the puzzle below. Answers may be horizontal, vertical, diagonal, or backwards.

```
X I T O G J L M Q A Q W E L
A C H I N C B A A E X N B H
F O R G I V E N E S S I O U
L K J H S K U Y T R E W O P
T Y B Y S E M N F V V C R R
F R Y I E T T R E Y A R P P
X D R E N I U Y L G H J K L
P F A I T H F U L N E S S Z
O A C H I J L M O Q A Q W E
A E I O W X N B W H T G H J
L N Y J Y D U T S E L B I B
G U Y T R E W Q H W E C B A
F R Y I C O M M I T M E N T
I U Y T G H J K P L P Q N S
```

Prayer	Commitment
Bible Study	Tithing
Faithfulness	Fellowship
Witnessing	Forgiveness

Find Joy in Faithfulness (vv. 5-10)

My family and I were living in Germany the year the Berlin wall came down. At about the same time Romania threw off communist rule and opened its borders to visitors from the west. Our church, the International Baptist Church of Stuttgart, collected and sent aid to the churches of western Romania. I was part of the team that drove the Bibles, food, clothes, and medicine to Oradia and several smaller Romanian cities.

While there I learned how the former rulers of Romania had persecuted the church severely. Meeting times had been tightly regulated. Neither Bibles nor any other Christian literature could be printed or imported. Evangelism outside the church was illegal. Pastors were categorized as unemployed and the children of Christian workers were discriminated against in education and employment. In these and many other ways the government had done all it could to discourage believers and empty the churches. Yet every church we visited was full to the point of overflowing. Why?

These believers had suffered greatly. But they found truth and meaning in their oneness with Christ. They knew suffering could not rob them of their victory in Christ. Also they found strength and encouragement in fellowship with other believers. As a result, even in the midst of such difficult times, their faithfulness brought them joy. We too found joy as we celebrated their faithfulness.

Learning Activity 2

SUFFERING AND PERSECUTION

1. How have you suffered for Christ's sake?

2. How has persecution tested, confirmed, or refined your faith?

3. How has God helped you in times of persecution?

Paul knew the Thessalonians would experience persecution but he didn't know how well they would endure it. To find out he sent Timothy back to Thessalonica. Had the new believers stood firm in the Lord? Did they blame Paul for their problems? Had they retreated to Judaism or to idolatry? Had all the missionaries' labor produced an enduring and growing church? Or had all their work just been wasted effort?

For Your Consideration (3:5-10)

1. What cause for joy did Paul see in the church's situation?

2. What did Paul hope to accomplish either through Timothy or by visiting the church again himself?

3. Do you think Paul's sympathy for others was lessened by the fact he had suffered so much for the Lord? Why?

4. How could you explain to a non-Christian the joy that can come from faithfulness in the face of affliction?

Paul thought he knew the answer but he had to be certain. Timothy's report confirmed Paul's expectations. True faith had rooted, grown, and produced in these believers the fruits of faithfulness and love. They had developed a maturity in the Lord that persecution could not destroy.

Today also growing Christians face various persecutions. Still they can find peace and joy not in surrender but only in continued faithfulness—even if continued faithfulness results in continued persecution.

The Thessalonians' faithfulness also gave Paul joy. Because of his love for them he celebrated their spiritual growth. Parents know how intensely they share the successes and the failures of their children. Spiritual parents (like Paul and like us) are much the same. Because we care about our spiritual children, or parents, or our brothers and sisters in the Lord, we share the joy of their successes and are saddened when they stumble. Love is like that.

Paul's example reveals that mature believers naturally care about the spiritual health of those around them. They want others to progress in the Lord. They go out of their way to encourage others. They pray for continued growth and do all they can to help others mature. If such an attitude is a sign of spiritual maturity, who are the mature believers in your church? Are you one of them?

Count on God's Blessings (vv. 11-13)

Over the years I have known many pastors and deacons concerned about the spiritual health of their congregations. Leaders try their best, but will their best be good enough? The answer of course is no. As important as our efforts are, they are never enough apart from the power of the Lord.

For Your Consideration (3:11-13)

1. What were the main elements of Paul's prayer for the Thessalonians?

2.. What kind of attitude should believers have toward all people?

3. Why didn't Paul pray for the Thessalonians' afflictions to end and never come back?

4. In what ways could your faith grow because of affliction endured?

5. If a person enduring affliction asked you to pray with him or her, how would you pray?

Keep On Growing

(1 Thess. 3:11-13)

Your Notes

Paul thus concluded his call for faithfulness and growth in the Lord with a prayer. He expressed three main concerns. First, he asked that the Lord would allow him to revisit Thessalonica. Satan had thwarted his best plans and efforts but Paul was not ready to give up. Instead he chose to continue planning and trying and to place the results in the Lord's hands.

Second, Paul prayed God would increase the Christian love among the Thessalonian believers. Paul called love the greatest Christian virtue (1 Cor. 13) and listed it first among the fruit of the Spirit (Gal. 5:22). Christlike actions grow only out of Christlike love.

Third, as the result of this abundant love, Paul prayed God would establish a blameless and holy people. To be without blame is to be acceptable before God. To be holy implies both having a relationship to God and living a life shaped by the commands of God.

This prayer reminds us that God's children always stand in submission to the Father. His will and ways are to shape our lives. This prayer also reminds us that God cares for us. He desires to guide us, empower us, and bless us. As we grow in the faith, we can always count on His blessings.

---

[1] Johann Christoph Friedrich von Schiller, *The Maid of Orleans,* last lines, (1801), as quoted in John Bartlett, *Familiar Quotations* (Boston: Little, Brown and Company, 1992), 365.

CHAPTER 4

follow God's will

Scripture Verses	• **1 Thessalonians 4:1-12**

Do you know God's will for your life? Discussions of God's will often focus on the occasional major decisions of life. Where should I attend college? Should we get married? Should I take that job? Should I commit myself to vocational Christian ministry? Should I retire now? If so, then what should I do?

Such major decisions deserve careful, prayerful thought. Yet our Father's influence should not be limited to those few pivotal moments. God cares about how you and I live (in other words, has a "will" for us) at all times. Are you doing God's will today?

Do you think of God's will as something hidden and hard to discover? Sometimes we do have difficulty knowing exactly what the Lord wants us to do. Yet in many ways the Lord's will is not obscure at all but fully revealed. Repeatedly in Scripture we find God's will for us clearly stated. All that remains is our obedience.

For example 1 Thessalonians 4 states the Father's will for His children. Obviously these verses do not cover all of life. But the passage does give some guidance in several areas of daily living. It also raises an important question: Are you obeying the revealed will of God in your life?

If we do not obey God's will revealed in Scripture, what makes us think we will obey God's will revealed through times of prayer? But if we are faithful to obey His revealed will, then obeying Him in difficult and pivotal moments should come naturally.

(1 Thess. 4:1-2)

Obey (vv. 1-2)

My son recently showed me a key chain he had just bought. It featured four small metal cubes in a row, each with a letter inscribed. The letters: WWJD.

"Do you know what they stand for?" he asked. I knew my first guess, "Wild Weird Juvenile Delinquent?" was both wrong and did not describe my son.

"No!" he laughed, "What Would Jesus Do? Have you ever heard that saying?" I admitted I had, when I read a book entitled *In His Steps*. I'm glad he wanted to carry this reminder of his commitment to follow the teachings and example of Jesus.

Do you ever ask yourself, What would Jesus do?

First Thessalonians 4 contains instructions for the church. The focus on the present in this and the next chapter distinguishes them from the first three chapters, which reflect primarily on the past. By calling us to obey, the first two verses of chapter 4 provide a foundation for the more specific commands that follow.

For Your Consideration (4:1-2)

1. According to verses 1-2 what can a believer do to please God?

2. How does a person grow in obedience?

3. How might you change your daily behavior so it is more pleasing to God?

These Christians already knew about the behavior God expected. Paul had explained to them how Christians are to live and the kind of life that pleases God. In 4:1 he affirmed and challenged them. They already had started living to please God but they could "excel still more."

Notice that verses 1-2 are encouraging and forward looking. We can affirm people who are making a genuine effort, even though they are not perfect, even though they fail at times. Criticism alone is discouraging. Even a well-meaning challenge to "do better" can feel like a reprimand unless we balance it with honest

Learning Activity 1

THE WILL OF GOD

1. Why is it difficult to know God's will in certain situations?

2. Think of a time when you were not certain of God's will and stepped out in faith. How did God reveal His will in that process?

3. What are you dealing with now where you are uncertain of God's will?

4. How can you become more certain of God's will in this situation?

(1 THESS. 4:3-8)

recognition of the good a person has done or the growth they have shown.

God's will is for Christ's commands to shape our thoughts and our actions. If we claim Jesus as our Lord, then we obligate ourselves to obey His teachings. We all know this. But we also need a reminder from time to time. As we each seek to obey Him, we also can seek to affirm godliness in others and encourage the entire church to excel even more.

Be Pure (vv. 3-8)

What is sanctified living? A thing or person sanctified has been made holy and belongs to God. For instance, the vessels in the temple in Jerusalem were sanctified and so were to be used only for the worship and glory of the Lord. You and I are called to live as those who have been made holy and who belong to God.

Sanctification impacts the whole of life but this passage focuses on moral (especially sexual) purity. God wills that we "abstain from sexual immorality." We understand that but what about "possess . . . [one's] own vessel"? Does this mean to manage one's own body or sexual urges and so act in a godly way? Or does it refer to the marriage relationship and mean for a husband to live with his wife in a godly way?

For Your Consideration (4:3-8)

1. On the basis of 4:3-8 how would you describe a sanctified Christian life?

2. Why can a believer never afford to ignore the Scripture's call for sanctification?

3. How does sanctified sexual behavior contrast with ungodly sexual behavior? List several differences.

4. How might a person defraud another in terms of business or in terms of a sexual relationship?

5. What behaviors does the world consider acceptable but the Lord labels immoral?

Socially accepted immorality

Either way, the two phrases "in sanctification and honor" and "not . . . like the Gentiles" dominate the passage. Sexual behavior in all situations should be governed by our relationship with God and by our desire to respect and obey His will. Have you given your sexuality to God? Is your sexual behavior guided by His values and His commands?

To answer these questions yes, you will avoid three kinds of sexual behavior. (1) Sexual behavior guided by nothing but self-gratification. Sexual desire is natural and of God. But "lustful passion" implies a self-centered, self-absorbed kind of desire contrary to the nature and will of God. (2) Sexual behavior heedless of the will of God. If God does not govern your actions, then something or someone less than God will. The results will be living that's less than godly. (3) Sexual behavior that ignores the value and rights of other people.

Paul warned believers about transgressions against others "in the matter" (v. 6). "The matter" could refer to sexual behavior but it often related to business in general. In either context—a sexual relationship or a business relationship—Christians are to demonstrate holy living.

YOUR NOTES

(1 THESS. 4:9-10)

"I will keep pure and holy both my life and my art"[1] is good not only for physicians but also for Christians. God called us not to impure but to sanctified living. Thus God's will is for us to live pure and holy lives. If instead we live in a way that flaunts God's commands, we are rejecting Him, resisting His Spirit, and risking judgment.

Love (vv. 9-10)

God's will also is that we love one another. We know God has taught us "to love one another." How has God taught us about love? Look first in the Old Testament and its description of how He treated His chosen people. There God has shown that genuine love commits fully, rejoices in the relationship, and endures faithfully.

In Depth

According to 1 Thessalonians 4, God's will is for us to

a. live a sanctified life (vv. 3,4,7)
b. abstain from immorality (v. 3)
c. refrain from defrauding others (v. 6)
d. practice godly love (v. 9)
e. earn the respect of outsiders (v. 12)
f. provide for our own needs (v. 12)

God also taught us love through His Son. The word for "love" was not very prominent in Greek usage. The word's rich meaning comes from the New Testament's description of the undeserved, sacrificial, and total love of God revealed in Christ.

For Your Consideration (4:9-10)

1. How did Paul know the Thessalonians were growing in love?

2. What do you think the Thessalonians were doing to show their love toward others in Macedonia?

3. In what ways do you practice love toward others?

Bob Carroll has served as the pastor for the people of Petaluma Valley Baptist Church (in California) for 20 years. At a recent anniversary celebration past and present members of the church shared their most lasting memories of Bob. Most often told were tales of Bob's service inspired by his love for God's people.

In Depth

Other New Testament passages to consult about God's will:

a. Mark 3:35
b. Romans 12:1-2
c. Ephesians 6:6
d. Hebrews 10:36
e. 1 Peter 2:13-15
f. 1 John 2:17

One man wept as he recalled the car accident that left his mother hospitalized and in a coma six hours away from their Petaluma home. But what brought tears was his memory of Bob driving repeatedly from Petaluma to his mother's bedside to sit, hold her hand, and pray. After six weeks the woman woke. She knew nothing of the unnumbered hours Bob had dedicated to her. But her family will never forget his loving sacrifice on their behalf.

Have you served others motivated by a sacrificial love? God's will is for us to love one another. Not with a shallow, earthly love but with a love that echoes both the deeds and teachings of Jesus. Such love is of God; and we are all challenged to "excel still more" (v. 10) in love than we have in the past. Are you growing in love? If so, then you have discovered a significant part of God's will for your life.

YOUR NOTES

(1 THESS. 4:11-12)

Work (vv. 11-12)

One snowy winter day when I was small, my family drove from our home in Dallas, Texas, to my grandparents' home in Nacogdoches. The normal 3-hour drive through East Texas lasted over 10 hours due to a freak ice storm.

In one town along the way, a steep hill had iced over and cars littered the ditches on both sides of the road. We made it up the hill for only one reason. By the time we arrived there several local residents had seen the problem and stationed themselves on the sides of the road. They threw dirt on the new ice; they pushed and pulled and got us past an obstacle that should have stopped us cold. Since then we never pass through that town without feeling a sense of gratitude.

Learning Activity 2

THE WORLD'S VIEW

1. How does the world view Christians?

2. How does the world's view of business, politics, and domestic life differ from the Christian's view?

3. As believers, how can we be better examples for the world to follow?

For Your Consideration (4:11-12)

1. What three things did Paul command the Thessalonians to do?

2. What do you think Paul would say about people who cannot provide for themselves?

3. What can you do to gain the respect of your community and so strengthen your witness in it?

Believers are to position themselves so they can help people in need. When believers do that, they earn the respect of their community. As a result their witness will get a fair hearing and their work for the kingdom of God will not be hindered. Also believers are to work to provide for their own material needs—since a believer in need will have difficulty being able to help others.

Verses 11-12 elaborate on the command to exhibit God-taught love. But the focus shifts from Christians' relationships to one another to their relationships to non-Christians. Because of God-taught love Christians are to live as respectable and productive members of their communities.

What is God's will for your life? Maybe you can't answer that question fully yet. But you can know the revealed will of God. His will is recorded for all to read in these and other verses in His Word. Reading and discovering His will sets the stage for another important question we each should ask ourselves: As far as I know, am I obeying God's will for my life?

[1] Hippocrates, *The Physician's Oath,* Translated by W. H. S. Jones in the *Loeb Classical Library* as quoted in John Bartlett, *Familiar Quotations* (Boston: Little, Brown and Company, 1992), 71.

CHAPTER 5

find comfort in the Christian hope

Scripture Verses	• **1 Thessalonians 4:13-18**

Referring to a frail ninety-year-old man he baptized two years earlier, my pastor announced: "Last Sunday as he left the service Mr. Leet said, 'See you next Sunday, pastor.' And I looked forward to it because he always had an encouraging word to say and brightened my day. Well, Mr. Leet died last week."

The congregation groaned its sadness. But the pastor wasn't finished. "And though I miss seeing him, I'm convinced he is with us this Sunday too, much as he planned. But now he is a part of that great crowd of witnesses voicing words of encouragement, urging us to be faithful and finish well our race."

The loss of a loved one through death is a traumatic experience. But in the midst of loss and grief believers can find a measure of comfort. A child of God has the assurance that the death of a fellow believer does not cause a permanent loss but a temporary separation. The departed loved ones are safe with the Lord and ultimately we—together with them—will know the joy of reunion and the glories of heaven.

Paul knew and shared the comfort of this promised future with his churches. The promise of resurrection robs death of its sting (1 Cor. 15:54-58). The truth of the Lord's return promises a grand reunion.

Grief and Hope (v. 13)

Accurate knowledge can calm many fears. Is a mechanic likely to suffer a panic attack when his car needs repair? Would you expect a pediatrician to rush to the emergency room because her child is showing the symptoms of a common and curable childhood disorder? Of course not! People are often frightened by the unknown or by things they do not understand. Paul did not want members of the Thessalonian church to be "uninformed . . . about those who are asleep." Thus he reminded them of some important and helpful truths.

People today often say someone "passed away" rather than use the harsher sounding term *died* (especially around family members). Those in the ancient world used "asleep" in much the same way. An example is found in 1 Thessalonians 4:13.

Learning Activity 1

SEEKING COMFORT

1. One way I draw comfort from music during a time of loss is

2. During a time of grief God speaks to me through prayer and

3. I can seek comfort from God's Word by

For Your Consideration (4:13)

1. What purpose did Paul hope to accomplish with the teachings in these verses?

YOUR NOTES

(1 THESS. 4:13)

2. Paul must have told the Thessalonians previously about the resurrection. Why do you think they needed this reminder?

3. What could you do to help someone who has "no hope"?

Paul wanted to help the church members deal with death. He offered the Christian hope as comfort: in Christ, believers can look forward to resurrection and ultimately to reunion with departed loved ones. Thus they need not grieve as people who do not have this hope. In the New Testament hope is not simply a fond wish that is uncertain of fulfillment but the confident anticipation of a future promised by the Lord.

In Depth

Major New Testament passages about the end times:

a. Mark 13
b. Matthew 24—25
c. 1 Corinthians 15
d. 1 Thessalonians 4:13—5:11
e. Revelation 1—22

This does not mean believers should not grieve at all. A personal loss, even a temporary loss, is valid cause for grief. Paul's desire was to comfort and we are to seek to do the same. In presence as much as by word we remind fellow believers of the love of God and of the sure future in His kingdom that we all share.

Assurance (v. 14)

Paul saw the resurrected Jesus on the road to Damascus and his life was changed forever. For Paul, the resurrection proved Jesus was the Son of God. Jesus' resurrection also proved His victory over sin and death. Jesus' conquest of death proved His power to provide resurrection to His followers.

"If we believe," as stated in Greek, assumes the fact of that belief. Since Jesus died and rose, we know He has power over sin and death. He promised eternal life to His disciples, so those who have died in Christ are still alive in Him. In addition, when Jesus returns, He will bring with Him all those believers "who have fallen asleep." This is no abstract discussion of the end times. Rather it assures believers of their resurrection and reminds them of the future reunion of all God's children.

For Your Consideration (4:14)

1. What assures believers that a day of resurrection is coming?

2. Why does Jesus' resurrection provide hope for believers?

3. What difference can a belief in the resurrection of Jesus make in the life of a person?

A friend recently lost her 18-year-old daughter. No, she didn't die. She joined the military and was shipped overseas. The separation is painful but is lessened by the assurance that eventually mother and daughter will be reunited. The promise of reunion dulls the pain of separation. Those who know Christ's promises can find hope in the twin promises of resurrection and reunion.

The Lord's Return (vv. 15-16)

The next three verses give more details regarding the Lord's return. We can be sure of these teachings because they came "by the word of the Lord." The Lord's return is not just Paul's opinion; it also is Jesus' promise. Thus the most important question to ask is not, Will He come? or even, When will He come? The most important question is, Am I ready for His certain coming?

YOUR NOTES

(1 THESS. 4:14-16)

FOR YOUR CONSIDERATION (4:15-16)

1. Whose authority was the foundation for Paul's teachings about the end times?

2. Why didn't Paul provide a detailed time line of end-time dates and events?

3. How does the sure return of the Lord change the way you deal with life?

Believers living at the time of the return will not "precede those who" have died. "Precede" implies both a priority in order and the gaining of an advantage. In other words Christians who die will be full participants in the dawning kingdom along with those believers who are alive when the Lord arrives.

The Lord's return will be trumpeted for all to hear. The "shout" is a "cry of command" either initiating the return or possibly calling for the resurrection of the dead (John 5:25). Who will

"The dead in Christ will rise first" (1 Thess. 4:16).

COURTESY OF KATHY C. FOLDS

utter the "shout"? If not Jesus, then the shout may be the same as the "voice of the archangel." The New Testament says little of archangels (see Jude 9) but the title implies a high ranking in God's angelic army. The trumpet also was an instrument of command, summoning or directing troops.

All three phrases—those related to the shout, voice, and trumpet—may describe a single heavenly command. If so, this combination is more stirring than any one description could be. Whether one sound or three, the end result is the same. The Lord's arrival is announced and "the dead in Christ will rise first." Their resurrection at the beginning assures that they precede the living as participants and will not miss a moment of the glory of that day.

Everlasting Reunion (v. 17)

After the dead rise, then the living "will be caught up together with them," and the living and the resurrected "shall always be with the Lord." The first part of verse 17 comments on the initial moment when all believers are "caught up" (or "raptured"). The last part of the verse immediately shifts to the eternal fellowship of all believers in the Lord. The promises of resurrection and reunion met the church's immediate need. Thus there was no need to discuss any events between the moment of the rapture and the joys of eternal fellowship.

But this approach leaves us with several questions. First, when will the rapture happen? The answer is we don't know. This verse—and indeed this passage—contains no hint or statement about that.

For Your Consideration (4:17)

1. What does verse 17 describe?

2. When are people best able to learn theological lessons—in the midst of grief, before a loss, or after the emotion of the moment has subsided? Why?

3. How does the guarantee of reunion with the saints and the Lord affect the way you look at death?

YOUR NOTES

(1 THESS. 4:17)

Second, what will happen immediately after all believers are raptured? Again Paul did not say. Some Bible students see the rapture as the removal of the church from the world. They believe the coming of the Lord in judgment will be a later and a separate event. Others think the rapture is a part of the Lord's coming, not a separate event that precedes His coming by several years.

COURTESY OF KATHY C. FOLDS

We can look forward to the future reunion of all God's children.

Third, if the rapture is not a part of the Lord's coming, how does it relate to other end-time events? Many link the rapture with a terrible seven years of tribulation that immediately precedes Jesus' return. But exactly how are the two related? Some believe in a pre-tribulation rapture—that God will remove the church from the world at the beginning of those troubled days. Some believe the church will endure the whole tribulation and then be raptured (called a post-tribulation rapture). Others think the Lord will remove the church three-and-a-half years after the tribulation begins (called a mid-tribulation rapture).

Nevertheless, this and other passages about the end times help the church live in the present. For instance, they teach us to live right today because a day of judgment and reward is coming. They teach us to endure today because (regardless of appearances) we are victors in Christ. These passages let us live with hope today, anticipating a grand reunion together and with the Lord. We do not have to know the details (or the sequence) of end-time events to benefit from such lessons.

Learning Activity 2

HOPE FOR THE FUTURE

1. What hope do you have concerning the future?

2. What assurance do you have of the resurrection of Christians?

3. Why does the promise of Christ's return provide comfort for you?

Application (v. 18)

Paul's intent was to comfort his readers in the face of death. He did so by assuring them of the resurrection. But even more he comforted them by pointing toward the assured reunion that is a part of the promised return of the Lord.

We believers still grieve at the loss of Christian friends and family. But our grief is the grief of temporary separation, not that of permanent and hopeless loss. The resurrection, rapture, and reunion are not just teachings about the future. They are truths that enable us to live with confident hope today.

For Your Consideration (4:18)

1. What did Paul intend believers to do with the teaching in these verses?

YOUR NOTES

(1 THESS. 4:18)

2. Why is the teaching in these verses comforting to a grieving believer?

3. How can you give comfort to someone who is grieving the loss of a Christian loved one?

"Don't be sad," said the well-meaning friend. "Your sister is better off with the Lord." As true as these words may be, they risk implying that believers who mourn the loss of a loved one have failed in their faith. We do not give comfort by shaming people into denying their grief.

How do you comfort people in the face of death? It isn't easy but time and again I have seen Christians inspired by love pay the price to minister as comfort givers. They sit; they cry; they reminisce; they pray. They help with mundane tasks. They may not feel they know what to say but their presence testifies without words to the love of God and the love of God's family for one another. Such presence is important. It reminds grieving believers they are not alone, that their loss is not the only reality in their lives, that God is a God of love and of hope, and that one day all of God's family will be gathered to celebrate a grand reunion. So let us celebrate this Christian hope. Let us comfort one another.

be ready for the future

Scripture verses	• **1 Thessalonians 5:1-11**

As the year 2000 approaches, many students ask me: Will Jesus return? and Will the 1,000-year reign mentioned in Revelation 20 begin in the year 2000? My honest answer is: I don't know and I don't believe anyone else does (except the Father). I also share with them a few interesting facts about our calendar.

First, the calendar we use is neither scriptural nor inspired. It is based on an early church calendar that made the year of Christ's birth the pivotal point for all history. The early calendar calls that year *Anno Domini* 1 (Latin for "in the year of [our] Lord"). Thus the first 1,000-year period was from the year 1 through the year 1000. The second millennium began on January 1, 1001 and concludes at the end of the year 2000. The third millennium will begin January 1, 2001.

Second, the calendar's creator made a mistake estimating the year of Jesus' birth. Later historians had more data and found that Herod the Great died in the year 4 B.C. Since Jesus was born before Herod died (Matt. 2:1,19), Jesus' birth must have been about six years earlier than first thought or about 6 B.C.

Accordingly the beginning of the third millennium A.D. is not the year 2001 (or the year 2000). The first thousand years after Jesus' birth would extend from 6 B.C. through A.D. 995. The second thousand then would extend from A.D. 996 through 1995. Since we are not absolutely certain of the exact date of Jesus birth, these figures could be off by as much as a couple of years. But even allowing for that uncertainty, the second millennium, figured from the year of Jesus' birth, ended no later than the end of 1997.

YOUR NOTES

(1 THESS. 5:1)

Is Jesus going to return 2,000 years after His first arrival? Well, if He hasn't come by the time this Bible study is published, the answer is no. Might He come in 2000 or 2001? Certainly. He will come whenever the Father wills. Should believers therefore be captivated by persons or groups claiming they have figured out when Jesus will return? Absolutely not! Jesus warned His disciples not to believe such people (Matt. 24:23-27,36-42).

The new millennium begins?

Since we can't predict it but are certain it will occur, what should we do about the return of the Lord? I'm convinced we should prepare for His arrival. That's how Paul counseled the Thessalonians. Are you preparing for the Lord's return? How?

Remember (v. 1)

Sometimes a pastor must teach new believers new things. Often the pastor simply must help Christians remember things they already have learned and challenge them to live as they know they should. Paul apparently thought the Thessalonians knew all they needed to know about "the times and the epochs" of the Lord's return. I doubt their curiosity was fully satisfied. I'm sure they didn't know all the details of the Lord's return or possess a schedule of end-time events. But does a believer really need such a schedule to live a healthy Christian life?

For Your Consideration (5:1)

1. What did Paul feel was lacking in the church's knowledge of the "times and the epochs"?

2. Why do you think believers need reminding of truths they already have heard? Do they forget, neglect, or rebel against these truths?

3. What do you think the church today absolutely must know about the day of the Lord?

In verses 2-11 Paul reminded the church that they knew the Lord would return, even if they did not know the day. They knew God would judge evil, even if they didn't know exactly when. They also knew God willed them to live each day guided by faith, hope, and love. If believers with such knowledge live on the basis of what they already know, they will be prepared for tomorrow, whatever tomorrow brings.

In Depth

Children of Darkness	Children of the Light
• Do not expect Jesus' return	• Expect the Lord's return
• Suffer a false optimism regarding the future	• Enjoy a valid optimism regarding the future
• Live unprepared for the coming judgment	• Live prepared for the coming judgment
• Will not escape the day of the Lord	• Act out faith, hope, and love
• Are destined for wrath	• Possess salvation

Rest Assured (vv. 2-3)

Do you have friends you can rely on? If they promise to do something, you know they will follow through. Well, the promises Jesus made to His church are even more reliable. One day as He promised He will return in glory and judgment.

YOUR NOTES

(1 THESS. 5:2-3)

Paul used two word pictures to describe the Lord's return. The first: "a thief in the night." How will Jesus' return be like the coming of a thief? Jesus isn't coming to steal. But just as the arrival of a thief, Jesus' return will be unexpected. "Suddenly" implies a surprise, an unexpected event. Unbelievers who think they are secure will suffer unexpected destruction because they cannot see in the darkness.

Readers often overlook the second word picture: the "woman with child." How does a woman's experience of labor compare to the Lord's return? I remember when my wife, Beth, entered her ninth month carrying our first child. She complained that I was watching her like a ticking bomb. Her labor pains were not unexpected but eagerly anticipated.

FOR YOUR CONSIDERATION (5:2-3)

1. What two images did Paul use to describe the coming of the Lord?

2. Since Paul did not give dates or details in this passage, why did he discuss the Lord's return at all?

3. What does the assurance that the Lord will return mean for unbelievers? for believers?

What is the point of the biblical analogy? The last clause of verse 3 gives us a clue: "and they will not escape." The coming of the Lord is as inescapable as labor at the end of a normal pregnancy. The day of the Lord, and the judgment that attends it, is inevitable and unavoidable.

Learning Activity 1

PARAPHRASING SCRIPTURE

Read the following Scripture passages and then paraphrase them in your own words.

1. Matthew 24:23-27

2. Luke 12:39-40

3. 2 Peter 3:10

The Lord is coming. Believers know this fact, even if those outside the church remain in ignorance and denial. The day of judgment cannot be avoided. Believers know this too. Because that day is coming, all people need to be prepared for it. Are you prepared?

(1 THESS. 5:4-10)

Live in Anticipation (vv. 4-10)

I live in earthquake country. The Rogers Creek fault zone is east of my house, the San Andreas to the west. Either could produce a devastating earthquake. Experts predict that one of them will do just that within the next 50 years.

What should I do? My mother says "Move back to Texas!" (and bring her grandsons with me). But the Lord has put me here at Golden Gate Seminary, so here I'll stay.

Since I'm not moving, common sense dictates that I prepare for the coming earthquake. Buy quake insurance. Keep enough water, food, and other supplies on hand. Be prepared to live with minimum assistance for several days. To do less would be foolish since I know the quake is coming one day.

Paul told the church the Lord was coming one day and he wanted them to be prepared. What he was inspired to write in verses 4-10 wasn't intended to satisfy idle curiosity about end times or provide hints regarding the date of the Lord's arrival. It does not even contain much detail about the Lord's return. But repeatedly and clearly the text reminds us to anticipate the day of the Lord.

Some will not be ready for it. Unbelievers are like persons who stumble about in the dark or those who are drunk or who are asleep. They cannot see where they are going. They are neither aware nor watchful. They have rejected Christ so they cannot live enlightened by salvation, His love, or His teachings. Tragically Christ's return will surprise them like the unexpected arrival of a thief. They will not escape the judgment but will suffer the wrath of God.

For Your Consideration (5:4-10)

1. How did Paul describe believers and unbelievers in verses 4-10?

2. What did Paul advise believers to do since they know the Lord will return one day?

3. Why might believers stop living in anticipation of the Lord's return and how might this failure affect their actions?

4. What kinds of problems would you expect in the lives of believers so focused on the future that they neglect their present Christian responsibilities?

5. How can a person move from darkness into light? What role can the church play in this transition?

6. What specific actions in your life are expressions of faith, hope, and love?

Christians, on the other hand, do not live in darkness. They know the Lord is coming but they don't know exactly when. So they will not be surprised as they would by a thief at night. As children "of the day" they expect His arrival. They also possess genuine hope, which consists of a confident expectation that the Lord will in fact return.

Christians are aware of the Lord's commands, which impact the way they live. They are to live sober and watchful lives. Likewise faith, love, and hope are to shape their actions and attitudes. These three core Christian virtues undergird the entire Christian life (1 Cor. 13:13).

YOUR NOTES

(1 THESS. 5:11)

Christian love values and deals with others as Jesus Himself did. People of hope eagerly anticipate the Lord's return and live as those who know for a fact that a day of reckoning and of reward is coming. Faith involves belief, commitment, and faithfulness.

Learning Activity 2

BUILDING UP EACH OTHER

In 1 Thessalonians 5:11, Paul admonished the Thessalonians to encourage one another. In today's world, we often feel as though we are treading water in a sea of negative comments.

Complete the following open-ended statements.

A word of encouragement makes me feel . . .

A word of criticism makes me feel . . .

One way I can encourage others is . . .

Predicting the date (even if it were possible) will not prepare a person for the return of the Lord—nor will selling all one has and retreating to some holy place to sit and wait. Those ready for Jesus' return have moved from darkness to light. They have received salvation by grace through faith in God's Son.

Their sins are forgiven and they need not fear God's wrath. The people who exhibit faith, love, and hope in their everyday lives, these are the only people prepared for the Lord's return—whenever it occurs. Are you prepared?

Encourage Others (v. 11)

The passage does not end with a prediction or with any unusual instructions or with a call for unique preparations. Instead it calls for caring and constructive Christian living. Just as Paul had encouraged believers, so also he called on church members to "encourage one another." Someone has said, "Believers should not worry about when Christ is coming, but should encourage one another because they are certain He is coming."[1]

"Build up one another" translates a verb used literally of constructing a building. Building up one another in the faith calls for constructive relationships in the church. Actions that divide fellowships and tear down other believers are exactly the opposite of what the verse calls for. Sadly, debates about the Lord's return sometimes have had this very effect, ending in hurts and divisions.

For Your Consideration (5:11)

1. What did Paul encourage the church to continue doing as they awaited the Lord's return?

2. How can the truth of the Lord's return serve as the justification for commands to encourage and edify the church?

3. What could you do to encourage and build up other believers?

How does a church prepare for the Lord's return? By living His love and sharing His truth. We may not be able to agree on the details of His return but we can all share the hope of His coming. We can encourage one another in the faith. We can act and talk in ways that build others up, not tear them down. We can live godly lives today so we will not be ashamed should the Lord return tomorrow.

[1] Quoted in Herschel H. Hobbs, *My Favorite Illustrations,* Ronald K. Brown, comp. (Nashville: Broadman Press, 1990), 232.

CHAPTER 7

persevere in Godly behavior

Scripture Verses	• **1 Thessalonians 5:12-28**

Have you ever helped build a church building? I have, on two different occasions. Both times I was a part of a volunteer, unskilled labor pool—we drove nails, painted walls, pulled wiring, and did whatever else was needed.

Both were real learning experiences. I learned working with volunteer labor can be hard. I learned the value of a good leader. I learned to value skilled coworkers. I also learned the value of a positive work environment. In the end we built more than a building; we built a stronger fellowship.

Building up the church body also requires working with volunteers. Likewise it requires good leaders who model faith. Mature workers willing to help the less experienced are needed too; so is an affirming and constructive atmosphere.

Are you helping to build up your church? First Thessalonians 5:12-28 calls for believers to act in ways that strengthen the church. It recommends actions that can produce a healthy, growing fellowship.

Support Good Leaders (vv. 12-13)

When children fail to appreciate what parents do for them, we may overlook it because they are immature. Thoughtless adults are a different matter however. Adults who cannot appreciate the work of others display troubling immaturity.

Church members are to appreciate and esteem their leaders. Quiet, diligent workers in the Lord's field sometimes labor for years with little more than an infrequent thank-you. Churches can exercise the discipline of noticing good behavior.

Leaders who conduct their ministries in a way consistent with the character and commands of Christ deserve the appreciation of the church. How does your church express high regard for its leaders?

COURTESY OF RICK BURTON

We can note good leaders who labor in the church. They work hard and consistently. Such leaders do not just possess a title; they faithfully perform work beneficial to the church they serve.

For Your Consideration (5:12-13)

1. What kind of leaders should a church highly esteem?

2. Why do churches often need a reminder to esteem good leaders?

3. How can you or your church express esteem for your church's leaders?

YOUR NOTES

(1 THESS. 5:12-13)

Leaders especially need the esteem of the church when they must correct some error or give instruction. Few people enjoy correction. Giving it is stressful. Receiving it is humbling. If done poorly, conflict can result. Yet none of us are flawless. So we all need to be corrected at times and those who bring us the Lord's instruction deserve our respect.

Learning Activity 1

Some Imperatives FOR YOU

An imperative is a command or a strong request. First Thessalonians 5:13-22 has 15 imperatives that instruct readers. Read the verses and write the imperative statements below.

1.
2.
3.
4.
5.
6.
7.
8.
9.
10.
11.
12.
13.
14.
15.

All believers should love one another and this includes their leaders. But good leaders earn an extra measure of love "because of their work."

A call for peace caps the passage. The people of God can resent godly admonition and fight with their leaders. Followers can divide into factions rather than work together. Building up the church requires peace. Are you an agent of peace in your church?

Help the Weak and Wayward (vv. 14-15)

I have taught in college and seminary since 1980 and have seen all sorts of students. After one trying day I joked with a friend that my job would be a lot easier if it weren't for students. Of course without students I would have no job. And if all students were fully informed and mature, they would have no need of a school like the seminary.

For Your Consideration (5:14-15)

1. Whom did Paul encourage believers to help?

2. Why do churches always seem to have a number of troubled or troublesome people?

3. What might a church do to provide help for unruly, fainthearted, or weak members?

The church is much the same way. We might wish for a fully mature and problem-free church. But one sign of a growing, healthy church is the presence of immature persons in its fellowship. Lamenting their presence is like a doctor lamenting the presence of sick people in the waiting room.

People with problems—whether their problems are spiritual, emotional, or physical—need help. Yet ministry to these people can be trying. They do not always respond well or quickly even to those trying to help them. So believers are to be "patient with everyone."

Patience can sound passive, like doing nothing. But the church is not to ignore people with problems. Instead we are to try to help them just as God helped us in our sin. We help by introducing them to Jesus, by showing them godly love, by not responding to evil with evil acts of our own.

Find Joy in the Lord (vv. 16-18)

Images of God painted in the Middle Ages often portray His wrath. With thunderbolt in hand He glares down on humanity, ready to send fire and brimstone to punish evil. God's wrath is real but His true desire for us was revealed when He sent His Son. God wants the best for us. This truth underlies the three brief commands in verses 16-18.

For Your Consideration (5:16-18)

1. What specific behaviors are mentioned as being God's will for believers?

2. What might discourage believers from behaving in these three ways?

3. How might a church make these behaviors a regular part of worship and fellowship times?

Believers know God's power and love. He has welcomed us into His family and given us a sure future. Thus we rejoice, pray, and give thanks. God wants us to have a life of joy, full of reasons to offer thanks and sincere worship to Him.

This passage does not tell us to celebrate the evil that causes our pain or to rejoice in the pain itself. We can celebrate because we know that no earthly disaster can separate us from our Father or rob us of our inheritance in Him. At all times and in all circumstances we have reason to rejoice, worship ("pray" implies worship), and give thanks.

Learning Activity 2

TAKE A MOMENT

1. Read 1 Thessalonians 5:23-24. Write your own paraphrase of verse 23 in the space below.

2. After writing the paraphrase, review what you wrote. Reflect silently on how you are doing in fulfilling the verse in your spiritual journey.

Follow Spiritual Wisdom (vv. 19-22)

The two ladies in my office were angry. They had believed and sent large offerings to a TV preacher. When he was exposed as a fraud, they felt inclined not to trust any preacher. Their reaction to feeling gullible was to become cynical. But if the gullible err by accepting lies they assume are true, the cynical err by rejecting truth they assume is a lie. Neither is healthy.

(1 THESS. 5:19-22)

Paul knew false teachers would infiltrate the church and he argued against false teachings in several letters. Yet the true gospel is also proclaimed in the church and the people need to remain open to hear the Word of God.

FOR YOUR CONSIDERATION (5:19-22)

1. How should a church respond to persons claiming to speak spiritual truths?

2. What might happen if a church stops exercising spiritual discernment and blindly follows self-appointed leaders?

3. How could a person or church "quench the Spirit"?

The two parallel statements in verses 19-20 urge the church to remain open to the Spirit of God. Christians who don't "quench the Spirit" or "despise prophetic utterances" can hear spiritual truth. Through Spirit-led messages they learn God's truth for His church.

In Depth

According to 1 Thessalonians 5:12-28 we build up our church when we

1. affirm and follow spiritual leaders (vv. 12-13)
2. pursue a peaceful fellowship (v. 13)
3. persevere in ministry to the needy (vv. 14-15)
4. always seek the well-being of others (v. 15)
5. retain our joy in the Lord (vv. 16-18)
6. exercise spiritual discernment (vv. 19-22)
7. rest in the power of God (vv. 23-24)
8. maintain a loving church family (vv. 25-27)

The church also is responsible to listen with discernment. Anyone can claim to speak for God. Truth and error still compete today for people's attention even in churches. Discernment is essential if believers are to avoid error and the church is to be built up.

Depend on the Lord (vv. 23-24)

The computer Golden Gate Baptist Theological Seminary provided for my use is a marvelous machine running excellent Bible study and word processing programs. But without power it would be nothing more than a useless pile of parts.

Similarly Paul gave marvelous advice in this passage aimed at promoting the health and growth of the church. But he knew the best processes and programs were futile apart from the power of God. So the prayer at the end of the letter highlights God's provision for the work of the church and in the life of the individual believer.

For Your Consideration (5:23-24)

1. Who is the source of sanctification and preservation for Christians?

2. Why does 1 Thessalonians urge believers to live in a sanctified manner (4:3-7) and then express a prayer for God to sanctify believers?

3. What signs in your life indicate God is sanctifying you?

The prayer consists of two requests and an assurance. The requests were for God to sanctify and to guard or protect the believers. We who seek to obey God should not think we can do so in our own power. God is the One who sanctifies. He also preserves us. Our entire being is secure in His hands.

This prayer assures us of God's faithfulness. God will do what He has promised. Can we do less than respond with faithful obedience?

Closing (vv. 25-28)

A series of brief commands conclude the letter. First, Paul asked these "brethren" to pray for him and his fellow workers. A church family should remember to lift up one another in prayer. Who else would know better specific needs or reasons for praise?

Friends and family greet each other in a variety of ways in various cultures. Some kiss, others hug, bow, or shake hands. The "holy kiss" likely calls for believers to express mutual love in a genuine, affirming fashion.

For Your Consideration (5:25-28)

1. What three things did Paul tell these believers to do for one another?

2. Which of the three things helps you most? Why?

3. How can you help other believers hear the message of 1 Thessalonians?

Paul next expressed his concern for other believers to hear the message directly. No priests stood between the people and their God or His messengers. Equal access to the Word implies equal responsibility to obey the Word.

Ordinary letters of the first century ended with a simple "farewell." Paul lifted the eyes of his readers higher. The final, memorable note he struck was of the grace of Jesus Christ. For those who know Jesus, such a conclusion calls for perseverance in godly behavior.

CHAPTER 8

trust God

Scripture Verses	• **2 Thessalonians 1:1-12**

I have an Iranian friend, now living in England, who was converted from Islam. He returns to Iran regularly to encourage a small church there. If caught engaging in evangelistic activity, which is illegal there, he will be imprisoned.

Several years ago I visited with some missionaries of our International Mission Board. They live and work in a country that religiously is dominated by another denomination. Working through the government, this church had succeeded in having "proselytizing" outlawed. Southern Baptist missionaries there risk serious punishment when they witness outside their church buildings, especially to a minor.

We often take our religious freedoms for granted. In countries outside America, however, churches frequently struggle under strict regulation. Would you continue as a church member if it meant loss of prestige or property? If witnessing could result in your going to prison, would you witness? If anti-Christian forces had the upper hand, would you question God's presence, power, or love?

The Thessalonians faced persecution for their faith. Paul tried to help them understand what persecution meant, both for believers and for their persecutors. In a day when evil seemed to be winning, these believers needed to understand another day was coming when evil would receive its just reward.

Your Notes

(2 Thess. 1:1-2)

Greetings (vv. 1-2)

The greetings in both 1 and 2 Thessalonians are very similar. They are patterned after an ordinary Greek letter. There is one difference however between these two greetings. The greeting in 2 Thessalonians is expanded to highlight the source of grace and peace: "God the Father and the Lord Jesus Christ."

For Your Consideration (1:1-2)

1. How does this greeting compare with the greeting in 1 Thessalonians?

2. Do you think peace is something we create or something God gives us through His grace? Why?

3. How has God's grace brought peace in your life?

Grace, which is unearned favor, and peace, the presence of well-being, do not belong only to problem-free churches. The Thessalonians endured persecutions (1:5-10). False teaching disturbed the fellowship (2:1-11). Some members created problems that needed correcting (3:6-15). Yet this troubled church still had access to the grace and peace of God.

Churches today too face a multitude of problems. Few churches (if any) will ever be trouble free. So how can a church with troubles enjoy God's grace and peace? Only by realizing grace is not earned by defeating opponents and peace is not achieved by resolving all conflicts. Grace and peace come from trusting the Father who loves His children and from following Jesus who is Lord of all. God's peace can reign within us even while problems and persecutions swirl around us. Has God's grace brought you peace?

Thanksgiving (vv. 3-4)

Several problems threatened the peace and the health of the Thessalonian church. Assaults from outside the church were not the only threat to the congregation. Persons inside the fellowship also were creating conflict and confusion. Yet Paul did not require perfection before providing praise.

For Your Consideration (1:3-4)

1. Paul expressed thanks for the Thessalonians for what three reasons?

2. Why do you think Paul felt obligated to give thanks?

3. How does a person's life change when he or she grows in faith or love?

Someone has said, "Unexpressed gratitude is like winking at someone in the dark. You know how you feel about them, but they don't."[1] Paul expressed thanksgiving to God for these Christians in Thessalonica. He even boasted about them to other churches.

COURTESY OF KATHY C. FOLDS

(2 THESS. 1:3-4)

The Thessalonians continued to grow in faith and love. They were not flawless but they persevered in spite of "persecutions and afflictions." No wonder Paul spoke "proudly" of them!

Paul felt obligated to praise this church. Their actions had earned this affirmation. But the affirmation also served as encouragement. Honest words of praise can have a powerful, positive effect in the church today as well. Yet some church people seem to specialize in finding flaws and rebuking failures. We all know that flaws abound even in good churches; but faith, love, and perseverance exist too. These positive characteristics deserve encouraging expressions of praise. How do you deal with people?

Learning Activity 1

COMMITMENT OR TALK

A guest had preached that morning in Sam's church. As Sam drove home and reviewed the sermon, he thought, *It would have been a good sermon if I didn't know the speaker so well.*

Read 2 Thessalonians 1:3 and answer the following questions.

1. What are my friends and family saying about my spiritual life?

2. What changes do I need to make to be more like the Thessalonians and less like the speaker in the story?

My ministry often involves the evaluation of others. As a teacher I am required to critique students. As interim pastor

I often deal with churches in crisis. As a father I do my best to guide the growth of two teenage sons. In all these roles I have found honesty is essential. But being honest is not the same as being negative and harsh. A critical word may be correct but will leave a crushed spirit if it does not point past the problems to something better.

Reward and Punishment (vv. 5-10)

Do you ever get angry when the "bad guy" wins? I'm not talking about the movies. I mean in real life. Several years ago a friend told me he had a great idea for saving his company money. He submitted the idea to his boss who passed it along up the corporate ladder. Some months later a large monetary prize was awarded for this idea but not to my friend. It went to an executive's relative in the company who submitted the same idea. The relative's submission "just happened" to be dated one day earlier than my friend's.

Explaining the existence of evil would not have helped the Thessalonians deal with their afflictions. Instead they needed some important insights to help them to continue persisting in the faith. Note the five key ideas in verses 5-10.

For Your Consideration (1:5-10)

1. How will God eventually deal with persecutors and with the believers whom they persecute?

2. Who did Paul say would suffer the retribution of God and how did he describe that retribution?

3. Why do you suppose some people decide they must persecute the church and discourage others from following Jesus?

4. How can Christians try to prevent the eventual punishment of those who persecute them?

(2 THESS. 1:5-10)

First, suffering for righteousness' sake is evidence of the sufferer's righteousness. Believers do not seek suffering. But if we are persecuted because of our Christian witness, we at least can be sure our witness has been heard. We have been faithful and effective enough that an opponent felt the need to react. Since suffering for Christ testifies to our faithfulness, then suffering is "a plain indication" we are "considered worthy of the kingdom of God."

Learning Activity 2

TRUST IS RISKY BUSINESS

1. How is the phrase "trust is risky business" true in dealing with people?

2. How is the phrase "trust is risky business" not true in dealing with God?

3. What are some areas of your life in which you need to trust God?

4. Explain why you can trust God in everything.

Second, the suffering of the just at the hands of the wicked is evidence against the wicked. We may not see judgment, much less punishment, taking place now. We may not even see it in our lifetime. But God—who is the Judge and sees all—will "repay with affliction" any who afflict His people. The wicked earn their punishment and a just God will give them their earnings.

Third, the saved can look forward to eternal relief from all the temporary suffering they endure. But the wicked face eternal suffering for all the temporary suffering they have caused. Have you ever endured a temporary pain in order to secure relief from long-lasting pain? Having a root canal, for instance, is not a pleasant experience. But I would chose the temporary pain of a dental procedure any day over the long-term pain of an untreated tooth. The Christian's suffering is real and painful but it has a purpose and is temporary. The knowledge of certain and eternal relief can bring peace.

Fourth, those persons reaping "eternal destruction, away from the presence of the Lord" will suffer but not merely because they persecute the church. Persecution is only a symptom of a more basic sin. They have rejected God and His salvation through Jesus. Paul knew from personal experience that even one who persecutes the church can be saved. The best way to eliminate persecution is to tell persecutors how to become children of God.

In Depth

Five good reasons to give thanks to God (2 Thess. 1:3-10)

a. because Christians are growing in faith
b. because Christians are growing in love
c. because Christians are persevering in difficulty
d. because Christians are confident of Jesus' return
e. because Christians are assured of a glorious future

Fifth, the day of the Lord will be both a day of just condemnation and a day of wondrous glory. The images of "mighty angels" and "flames of fire" also stress condemnation and judgment on the evil ones afflicting God's people. Yet the same day will be a day of glory and wonder for "all who have believed." We endure the struggle because we love the Lord, trust Him, and look forward to sharing in the glory of His presence. We know we will share in the victory at the end.

Persevere in the faith. Remember your suffering is temporary. Accept affliction as evidence your faith is genuine and your witness effective. Know that those who reject the Lord and persecute the church will not escape their just reward and

(2 THESS. 1:11-12)

certainly will not win the day. Endure to the end, for the end will be a day of marvelous glory.

Prayer (vv. 11-12)

"You are not alone." How often these words comfort persons who are suffering. Believers comfort one another by sharing the burdens of life, including any persecution that comes. But believers are not limited to mutual support. They also can count on the presence and support of the living God.

The prayer in verses 11-12 reminded these Christians they had responded to God's call. Apart from that call and response they would have been lost. Paul prayed God would count them worthy. This term also can be translated "make worthy," stressing even more the role God plays in enabling Christians to live godly lives. Without the Father's grace and guidance and power, any person's efforts are futile. A life of goodness and faith, worthy of the calling to follow Jesus, grows out of the blended ground of (1) a disciple's genuine desire to serve God and (2) the Father's power to fulfill that desire by His grace.

FOR YOUR CONSIDERATION (1:11-12)

1. What did Paul pray would happen and what did he hope the result would be?

2. What does a person look like who is worthy of his or her calling in Christ?

3. What could a believer do to glorify the name of Jesus? (1:12)

Arrogance has no place in the life of a disciple. He or she does not seek personal glory but lives to glorify the Lord Jesus. Thus Paul prayed that Jesus would be glorified in the lives of the Thessalonians and that the Thessalonians would find their glory in Him.

COURTESY OF KATHY C. FOLDS

People are glorified when they are honored and their reputations are enhanced. Does your life honor Jesus? Do others (even unbelievers) see and respect His influence in your life? Some of the darkest days in believers' lives are days of affliction—days when evil seems to have the upper hand. When the light of the gospel shines forth from the lives of believers in such dark days, they have truly become the light in the darkness that Jesus expects of them (Matt. 5:14-16).

[1] Anonymous quote in Mark Link, *100 Stories for Special Occasion Homilies* (Allen, Texas: Tabor Publishing, 1992), 58.

don't be deceived

Scripture Verses	• **2 Thessalonians 2:1-17**

When is Christ going to return? No one except the Father knows but people keep trying to figure out the date or predicting when it will happen. The most recent prediction I read set March 31, 1998, as the time for Christ's return. Supposedly this would happen near Garland, Texas. When the date passed, there was a change of story.

Such failed predictions occurred many times before 1998 and there likely have been others since 1998. All of them, ironically, have had different timetables for Jesus to return. Yet these predictions have had at least one fact in common: they all have been wrong.

Sadly such predictions can distract the church from its work. Jesus Himself dealt with this problem even before His ascension. Acts 1:6 records the disciples' clamoring to know when Jesus would establish His kingdom. His response was simple and direct. First, the disciples could count on His return but they could not know the schedule. Second, they were to stop standing around looking for the return and get busy preparing for the return. Jesus called His disciples to be witnesses, not cloud-gazers. He wanted them to live each day prepared for tomorrow, not waste time dreaming about tomorrow.

The return of the Lord is important. We should study it. But we cannot allow such studies to distract us from the task Jesus gave us. Our task is not to predict His coming but to believe it, proclaim it, and prepare for it. Paul understood this and called for the same from the Thessalonians.

Some Teachings Are False (vv. 1-2)

Has rumor or gossip ever disrupted your church? Either malicious manipulation or innocent error can cause an uproar in a church. Paul did not want the Thessalonian church to be "shaken from" its "composure" or "disturbed."

TONY STONE

This description implies a double problem. One is the immaturity of a people who can quickly be thrown into turmoil. The other is the presence of persuasive and disruptive false teaching. One calls for encouragement. The other calls for correction. This chapter offers both.

For Your Consideration (2:1-2)

1. How did Paul describe the false teaching that was troubling the church at Thessalonica?

Your Notes

(2 Thess. 2:1-2)

2. What can happen to a fellowship that listens to false teachings?

3. How might believers today be shaken, disturbed, or deceived by false teachers?

The false teaching focused on "the coming of our Lord Jesus Christ and our gathering together to Him." The false teachers apparently claimed their teaching came by divine revelation and/or a letter from Paul. Since false teaching can fly under false colors, mature believers need to test for truth, not simply accept the teaching of everyone who claims to speak for God (1 Thess. 5:19-22).

A shaken, disturbed church can lose effectiveness. Divided over false teachings, fellowship suffers. Diverted from the gospel, doctrine suffers. Distracted by internal arguments, witness suffers. Could this happen to your church? The rest of 2 Thessalonians 2 tells us how to avoid this.

An ancient letter

ILLUSTRATOR PHOTO 390-27A

The Lord Is Coming (vv. 3-10)

How did false teachers try to show the day of the Lord had already come? We don't know. Paul focused on the timing of the Lord's return rather than on explaining the false teaching.

In Depth

The Day of the Lord in the Prophets—A Time of Judgment:

a. Isaiah 2:10-22; 13:1-22
b. Ezekiel 30:1-19
c. Joel 2:1-11,28-32
d. Amos 5:18-27
e. Zephaniah 1:7-18
f. Malachi 4:1-6

The term "day of the Lord" is used in several ways in Scripture. Here it apparently refers to the end times in a broad sense, including events leading up to the judgment. Did some in the church think their tribulations marked the beginning of the end? Was this why some were "doing no work" (3:11) and others were disturbed? Paul assured the church their circumstances did not mean the end had come. Yet he still wanted them to take a firm stand in the faith and so be ever ready for that day.

Paul reminded the church the stage was not yet set for the Lord's return. First, the apostasy would come, the "man of lawlessness" would be revealed and "he who now restrains" would be "taken out of the way." Since the Thessalonians knew about these things, there was no reason to explain them in detail. As a result many today debate the exact character of these events and their relationship to each other.

For Your Consideration (2:3-10)

1. What three events did Paul say must precede the coming of the Lord, and how do these relate to each other?

2. Why do false teachers try to mislead the faithful?

3. How should the promise of the Lord's ultimate victory affect the way people live today?

(2 THESS. 2:3-10)

"First" can leave the impression Paul had in mind events that would happen in sequence. But the details of the verses that follow suggest otherwise. For example verses 7-8 show the removal of the restrainer precedes the arrival of the lawless man. Thus rather than describing a sequence of events, this may refer to a single complex event that must occur first before the Lord's return.

Learning Activity 1

OUR LORD'S RETURN

Believers today can become more upset and disturbed over the second coming of Christ than perhaps any other subject. Read Matthew 24:4-8 for Jesus' warning against false signs of His coming. What does this passage teach you about our Lord's return?

"Apostasy" can describe a falling away from the church or a time of increased ungodliness in general as humanity rebels against God. Paul did not state which he had in mind. Both types of rebellion could occur. In such cases each feeds off the other.

Learning Activity 2

BELIEVING THE TRUTH

Read 2 Thessalonians 2:13-15 and answer the following questions.

1. How do the results of believing the truth differ from the results of embracing a lie?

2. What task did Paul instruct the believers at Thessalonica to do?

3. How does predicting the end time differ from preparing for the end time?

The identity of the restrainer is uncertain. The Greek word for "restrains" also can be translated "to hold" and has two possible meanings. The restrainer is either good and holds back lawlessness or is evil and now holds sway, dominating our fallen world until an even greater evil—the lawless one —takes over (1 John 2:18).

Most argue for a good restrainer holding back evil until God's appointed time. But who or what could this be? Some say rulers and governments that enforce rules of order. Others say the gospel and its evangelists who encourage the good in the world. A third possibility: an unnamed spiritual being, opposing Satan and inhibiting the growth of evil. Others identify the restrainer as the Spirit of God,

Your Notes

(2 Thess. 2:11-12)

God Himself, holding back both human and spiritual evil until a time set by His own authority.

The "man of lawlessness" describes a wicked person. He also is "Son of destruction," a term that marks him as one who is doomed. Thus the names define his character and his destiny.

The man of lawlessness is not identified and neither is a date suggested for his coming. We are not told how long the lawless one will be on the scene before Jesus will return. But this description does imply the presence of this son of destruction will be obvious to the church. Thus since the man of lawlessness was not then present, the day of the Lord had not yet arrived.

In Depth

In 2 Thessalonians 2 the man of lawlessness

a. is also called the son of destruction
b. aspires to divinity
c. is to be revealed at the proper time
d. is a persuasive satanic deceiver
e. has followers but they are doomed because they choose to reject the truth
f. will be destroyed at the return of Christ

Some Believe a Lie (vv. 11-12)

Sixty years ago Adolph Hitler was telling the German people they were a superior race and lesser races were to blame for their nation's troubles. He preached arrogance and hate. Those who embraced his lies were led down a path of escalating error. Fanatical loyalty to the lie eventually led to unbelievable atrocities.

For Your Consideration (2:11-12)

1. What will happen to followers of the "son of destruction"?

2. Why is not believing the truth equated with taking pleasure in wickedness?

3. Have you believed the truth? How do you know?

What happens when people embrace a lie? Romans 1:18-32 tells us about those who reject God and prefer the lie of worshiping other things. Their willful self-deception leads them down a path to a depraved mind and finally to destruction.

Even at the end of time some people will choose to reject the truth and believe a lie. Those who reject the truth, God will give over to the lie they have chosen, sending "upon them a deluding influence so that they will believe what is false." These are not believers but those who already have refused to believe the truth. Their commitment to "what is false" and their decision to take "pleasure in wickedness" justify God's judgment. For they chose the path that leads to their own destruction.

Some Believe the Truth (vv. 13-15)

Just as embracing the lie leads to destruction, devotion to the truth leads to salvation. Those in this church had received the truth; their task then was to "stand firm and hold to the traditions." "Traditions" refers to the body of teaching delivered by the apostles, the apostolic gospel. Rather than be disturbed by false teachings and disruptive human speculations about the end of time, these believers were to focus on the essentials of the faith. Paul counseled them to reject any teaching that conflicted with what the apostles taught. His advice is still good.

For Your Consideration (2:13-15)

1. What did Paul counsel the church to do in response to the false teaching?

2. Why was Paul optimistic about the church's ability to stand against error and evil?

3. When false teaching arises, how should mature believers react to it?

At the turn of the millennium religious speculations may run wild. Judge all such speculations by the teachings of Scripture. Some may claim to know when the Lord is returning. Jesus said only the Father knows (Matt. 24:36). Whom will you believe? Some may focus on predicting the end rather than preparing for the end. Which would Jesus have you concentrate on? (See Acts 1:6-8.) Some may forget salvation comes through "sanctification by the Spirit and faith in the truth" (2 Thess. 2:13), not by membership in some new cult. So hold firm to the faith today, persist in godly living today, and your Father will take care of your tomorrows.

Prayer (vv. 16-17)

Paul concluded his attempt to calm these Christians by turning their eyes to the Father and the Son. The love of God is certain, even in the most uncertain times. His grace offers us comfort and hope. And He is the source of our strength in difficult times.

FOR YOUR CONSIDERATION (2:16-17)

1. What three ideas about God do these verses emphasize?

2. Why do you think these three ideas are important to Christians today?

3. Besides salvation, how do Christians today experience God's love, grace, and comfort?

CHAPTER 10

keep on doing good

Scripture Verses	• 2 Thessalonians 3:1-18

If you knew Jesus would return next month, what would you do? Would you tell people the good news? Some might believe you. Others would not. Would you recognize with new clarity the limited value of material possessions? Yet you already know you should store up eternal rather than temporal treasures.

If you knew Jesus would return next month, would you change the way you live? No doubt, you should avoid jealousy, gossip, and immorality. Obviously you should pursue faithfulness and self-control and do good to others. In short you would want to hear Jesus say "well done" on the day of judgment.

Of course Jesus' followers should live holy lives but not just because we expect He will return soon. Believers are to exhibit holiness because we are new creatures in Christ (2 Cor. 5:17). His Spirit indwells us (Rom. 8:1-11) and His law is written on our hearts (Heb. 8:10).

The Lord's return is a blessed promise but whether He returns soon or delays for thousands of years, our calling remains the same. By His grace and power we are to follow Him and serve as His witnesses day by day (Acts 1:6-8). So this is our greatest challenge: not predicting tomorrow but serving today.

Pray for God's Power (vv. 1-5)

"Prayer Changes Things." I read these words many times on a sign over the baptistry in my home church. This simple yet powerful truth continues to nurture my daily walk

(2 Thess. 3:1-5)

with Jesus. Yet this truth also poses a question. Exactly what "things" should I expect prayer to change? circumstances? other people? me?

The request for prayer in these verses reveals some of what Paul expected prayer to change. It also reveals his attitude toward God to whom he prayed.

The first prayer request was "that the word of the Lord will spread rapidly." Paul certainly wanted people to pray for him and his companions but here he sought prayerful concern for the ministry more than for the missionaries personally.

The second request was that the gospel would be accepted. Paul did not just preach the gospel; he preached to people. So he asked for prayer that his hearers might accept the message.

The third request was for rescue "from perverse and evil men." At times evil people had hindered Paul's work and driven him away from responsive hearers (see Acts 13:50; 16:35-40). Deliverance from such people would leave Paul free to share the gospel.

For Your Consideration (3:1-5)

1. For what did Paul ask the Thessalonians to pray?

2. Why do you think evil persons sometimes hindered Paul's ministry even though he prayed for deliverance from such interference?

3. Which of Paul's prayer concerns are also valid for your life? What will you do about it?

God did not always rescue Paul from evil persons. When hindered in his travels or imprisoned away from his mission fields, Paul often wrote letters. I wonder if Paul ever realized that

God would use his letters to travel farther and convert more people than Paul personally ever could. Sometimes the Father answers our prayers in unexpected yet wonderful ways.

Meaningful prayer is a close relative of confidence in God and obedience to His will. Because the Lord is faithful, His children can approach Him with confidence. Yet those who come to the Lord must come with submissive hearts and a will to obey. Anything less makes a mockery of confessing Him as Lord. Do your prayers grow from confidence and bloom into obedience? If so, you know that obedience is not always easy. Often it requires the exercise of discernment and discipline.

Exercise Discipline (vv. 6-15)

"We were kicked out of our first church," said Dan (not his real name). I was surprised. He did not seem like a troublemaker. Dan explained that his wife was seen wearing slacks. He wouldn't make her stop dressing like that, so the deacons "disciplined" the couple for their "sin." Do you think Paul would have considered such action serious enough to justify exercising church discipline? What do you think was the goal of church discipline for Paul?

Before we answer that, we need to recognize the concepts that guided Paul here. (1) He was concerned for the church's purity. (2) Paul recommended discipline only when a sin persisted, was a public matter, and was defended as proper by the sinner. (3) Paul was concerned for the fallen believer.

Learning Activity 1

GODLY CHARACTERISTICS

1. Which characteristics of God do you find in 2 Thessalonians 3:3-5?

2. What are some negative or un-Christlike characteristics in your life?

3. What can you do to remove any negative or un-Christlike characteristics and incorporate godly characteristics into your life?

1. Avoid the Undisciplined (v. 6)

Paul warned the church to avoid associating with any believer whose life was unruly or contrary to apostolic teaching. "Who leads" translates a verb implying ongoing

Your Notes

(2 Thess. 3:6)

intentional behavior, not occasional error. The lifestyle of such a person conflicts with the Christian faith or "tradition." "Unruly" comes from a Greek word meaning "undisciplined" or "disorderly." Such a person may refuse to act as God expects or may act in inappropriate ways, such as by being a busybody.

For Your Consideration (3:6)

1. Whom did Paul instruct the church to avoid?

2. Why do you think Paul gave these instructions to the church?

3. What constitutes an undisciplined lifestyle today? Do you find any such elements in your life?

Christians are to exercise the discipline of distancing themselves from such behavior. They should not appear to condone the behavior of unruly persons by associating with them. They also should beware of the negative influence bad behavior can have on good people. The godly may never change the unruly but they can make sure the unruly do not change them. Bad behavior is contagious and serious cases sometimes call for quarantine.

2. Discipline Yourselves (vv. 7-10)

Following Jesus requires more than a passive, negative lifestyle based on a long list of thou-shalt-nots. Believers are to do what they know is right.

Paul had lived as an example of faith before the believers of Thessalonica. They could not follow the apostle's model and live like the lazy, unruly persons in their fellowship too. Thus church discipline includes mature believers' disciplining their own behavior.

What specific behavior did Paul model? First he did not act in an undisciplined manner. Some scholars think the unruly were idle because they expected Christ to return soon. But not even expecting Christ to come soon would have justified their behavior.

In Depth

As described in 2 Thessalonians 3, church discipline

a. is an expression of Christian love
b. shames the offender regarding his or her actions
c. involves the church disassociating from error
d. encourages disciplined, godly behavior by all
e. assumes continued ministry to the offender

Second, Paul neither forced nor exploited the generosity of others but rather he modeled the goodness of hard work and self-sufficiency. Paul did not want anyone to think he was just another traveling teacher selling a false philosophy to earn a living.

Third, Paul provided an example of consistency. He worked hard and honored hard workers. He also taught that those able but not willing to work should not be supported by others.

(2 THESS. 3:7-10)

FOR YOUR CONSIDERATION (3:7-10)

1. What kind of good example did Paul model for the church in Thessalonica?

2. Why did Paul choose to work for his living rather than ask followers to support him?

3. What kind of work ethic will believers have if they follow Paul's example?

3. Be Responsible (vv. 11-13)

This section directly addresses those leading undisciplined lives. These exhortations reprimand them for "doing no work at all, but acting like busybodies." This statement contains a word play on "work" and implies doing things outside the realm of meaningful work. The unruly spent their time in unnecessary or useless pursuits. Being "busybodies" is only one type of unproductive behavior they could have exhibited.

Jack Gulledge told about a mother's surprise for her three young children. When they returned home from school, she was marching outside their home with a picket sign. She was demanding that they accept more responsibility around the house, saying she wouldn't do any household chores until they agreed to change.[1]

For Your Consideration (3:11-13)

1. What did Paul command of the disciplined and undisciplined Christians?

2. How might people try to exploit the generosity of the church today?

3. How might a Christian avoid growing weary of doing good?

Paul wanted these believers to accept more responsibility and exhorted them to eat their own bread. To do so, they would have to work. The call to "work in quiet fashion" shows the unruly also inflicted another problem on this church. "Quiet" calls not just for silence but also for peace. Somehow the nonproductive activities of the unruly were disrupting the peace of the fellowship.

Faithful believers are not to respond to others' sins by becoming hard and unloving. Nor should they envy the false success of evil and follow it rather than Jesus. The wisest response to evil is continuing to do good, both because it is right and because it is a witness to those doing wrong.

Today as much as we might want to change someone else, we cannot do so. We can encourage others to change but change won't happen without their efforts. The same is true for us too. We also need to exercise the discipline of submitting to the Spirit and following the example of Christ. We too are to keep on doing good, even in bad situations.

4. Help Others Be Disciplined (vv. 14-15)

Believers witness by refusing to associate with those who are involved in bad behavior. The purpose of such action is to shame the believer and admonish him or her to live in a way consistent with the gospel. In other words the proper intent of church discipline is to help the one disciplined, not to punish the sinner or purge the church. The proper mood of discipline is love, not anger. The proper objectives of church discipline are to maintain the witness and restore the fellowship of the congregation.

YOUR NOTES

(2 THESS. 3:11-18)

FOR YOUR CONSIDERATION (3:14-15)

1. How did Paul want the church in Thessalonica to respond to the undisciplined?

2. What principles should govern a church's actions in disciplining a member?

3. What might a church do to help a wayward member return to a Christlike lifestyle?

Prayer (vv. 16-18)

This letter concludes with a prayer for peace, an assurance of genuineness, and an affirmation of grace. The persecutions from without and the controversy within made the need for peace evident. The prayer reminded the church that true peace does not depend on circumstance but is God's gracious gift to those who rest confidently in Him. The same remains true today. So as we too seek to obey His word and share His love, may we also find peace in His abundant grace.

FOR YOUR CONSIDERATION (3:16-18)

1. How did Paul verify that the letter was in fact from him?

2. Why do you think Paul concluded this letter with prayers for peace and grace?

3. How can a believer find peace in every circumstance?

[1]Jack Gulledge, *Ideas and Illustrations for Inspirational Talks* (Nashville: Broadman Press, 1986), 39.

Learning Activity 2

DEALING WITH THE UNDISCIPLINED

Read 2 Thessalonians 3:14-15. List four instructions Paul gave on dealing with the undisciplined.

1.

2.

3.

4.

Preparing Christians to Serve

In the **Christian Growth Study Plan (formerly Church Study Course),** this book ***Live for the Future Now: Studies in 1 and 2 Thessalonians*** is a resource for course credit in the **Developing Teaching Skills course (LS-0053) of the Leadership and Skill Development Diploma Plan and in the subject area Biblical Studies (CG-0490)** for the Christian Growth category of diploma plans.

To receive credit, read the book, complete the learning activities, show your work to your pastor, a staff member or church leader; then complete the information on the next page. The form may be duplicated. **Send the completed page to**

Christian Growth Study Plan
127 Ninth Avenue, North
Nashville, TN 37234-0117

FAX: (615) 251-5067

For information about the Christian Growth Study Plan, refer to the current Christian Growth Study Plan Catalog. Your church office may have a copy. If not, request a free copy from the Christian Growth Study Plan office (615/251-2525).

Please check the course(s) you want to apply this credit. You may check both. ☐ **CG-0490** ☐ **LS-0053 (Sunday School)**

PARTICIPANT INFORMATION

Social Security Number (USA ONLY)	Personal CGSP Number*	Date of Birth (MONTH, DAY, YEAR)
– –	– –	– –

Name (First, Middle, Last) ☐ Mr. ☐ Miss ☐ Mrs. ☐	Home Phone – –

Address (Street, Route, or P.O. Box)	City, State, or Province	Zip/Postal Code

CHURCH INFORMATION

Church Name		
Address (Street, Route, or P.O. Box)	City, State, or Province	Zip/Postal Code

CHANGE REQUEST ONLY

☐ Former Name		
☐ Former Address	City, State, or Province	Zip/Postal Code
☐ Former Church	City, State, or Province	Zip/Postal Code

Signature of Pastor, Conference Leader, or Other Church Leader	Date

*New participants are requested but not required to give SS# and date of birth. Existing participants, please give CGSP# when using SS# for the first time. Thereafter, only one ID# is required. **Mail to:** Christian Growth Study Plan, 127 Ninth Ave., North, Nashville, TN 37234-0117. Fax: (615)251-5067